A Substance Called Food

How to Understand, Control and Recover From Addictive Eating

Second Edition

Human Services Institute
Bradenton, FL

TAB BOOKS

Blue Ridge Summit, PA

Human Services Institute publishes books on human problems, especially those affecting families and relationships: addiction, stress, alienation, violence, parenting, gender, and health. Experts in psychology, medicine, and the social sciences have gained invaluable new knowledge about prevention and treatment, but there is a need to make this information available to the public. Human Services Institute books help bridge the information gap between experts and people with problems.

In the case histories cited, the author has used fictitious names and described traits not identifiable to any particular person unless that person has given express permission.

SECOND EDITION
FIFTH PRINTING

© 1989 by **Gloria Arenson**.
Published by HSI and TAB Books.
TAB Books is a division of McGraw-Hill, Inc.
First edition published 1984 by Rawson Associates, N.Y.

Library of Congress Cataloging-in-Publication Data

Arenson, Gloria.
    A substance called food : how to understand, control, and recover
    from addictive eating / by Gloria Arenson. — 2nd ed.
        p.   cm.
    Rev. ed. of: Binge eating, 1st ed. c1984.
    ISBN 0-8306-3430-4
    1. Eating disorders—Popular works.   I. Arenson. Gloria. Binge
eating.   II. Title.
RC552.E18A74   1989
616.85′26—dc20   89-20402
                                                                            CIP

TAB Books offers software for sale. For information and a catalog, please contact TAB Software Department, Blue Ridge Summit, PA 17294-0850.

Questions regarding the content of this book should be addressed to:

Human Services Institute, Inc.
P.O. Box 14610
Bradenton, FL 34280

Acquisitions Editor: Kimberly Tabor
Development Editor: Lee Marvin Joiner, Ph.D.
Cover Photograph: Susan Riley, Harrisonburg, VA

FOR BROCK

my partner and friend,
who has always known the
Truth about me
and inspired me to live it

"The life which is unexamined
is not worth living."
PLATO

BOOKS BY GLORIA ARENSON

How to Stop Playing the Weighting Game

ACKNOWLEDGMENTS

This book could not have been written without the help of the many wonderful people who have taken my classes and workshops and those who have shared their hopes and fears in individual counseling sessions. Special thanks are in order for the men and women who allowed me to use their words and experiences to help others still suffering.

Thank you my dear friends and colleagues Laurence T. Brockway, M.A., Eleanor Livingston, M.A., and Helen Powell, M.A., who have eagerly exchanged ideas with me and have been available for professional and personal support. In addition, I am grateful to Soloman Perlo, M.D., and Gretchen Newmark, M.A., for their valuable expertise.

I am happy to have had the assistance of Vickie Myers, Sarah Koolsbergen, and especially Bette Kramer in typing this manuscript and Sharon Zulauf, whose editing skills kept me to the point.

Contents

1

Food Addiction:
A Problem For
Millions

I HAD TO WRITE THIS BOOK

I have never met a woman who liked her body. Every woman I have ever known will go on at great length about her inadequacies: fat thighs, thick ankles, too small or too large a bust, small eyes, long chin, or fat earlobes. Women who are a size 20 dream of being a size 12; yet those who are a size 12 yearn to be an 8. No one seems to be satisfied, and this is the nature of the game. To chase the carrot of "someday I'll be perfect and then my dreams will come true" is what I call the weighting game.

As a psychotherapist and teacher I have dealt with thousands of women (anorectics, bulimics, and compulsive overeaters) who believe that if they change their appearance—get thinner—all their problems will be solved. They blame their unhappy relationships or lack of relationships on the premise that they are not slim enough to attract the right man or get the right job. Looking good equates with having a good life. It just isn't so!

Recently, I tried to remember a time in my life when I felt totally OK. When was it that I lived every day as it came, without feeling inadequate or worried about my future? When did my self-consciousness start? For me, it began at age twelve. Up until that time I *had* a body. After that I *was* my body. From then on, I was never at ease in the world. I had a handicap—my body—a body that would never be tall enough, slim enough, or flat-chested enough. Other women I know recall feeling unhappy about their bodies as young as three or four years of age.

Along with millions of other women, I have spent my life buying books and magazines that tell me how to improve. I have been obsessed with food, gone to doctors, clubs, self-help classes. All this energy was focused on hiding the not-OK feelings. After all these years, the magazines are still running the same articles, the books are rehashing the same ideas, and there are even more weight control businesses than ever before. Women are feeling more pressured and more frenzied in their efforts to achieve perfection that will lead to love and all the "happily ever after" dreams they cling to.

Five hundred million dollars are spent annually on diet products in the United States. We as a nation are obsessed with thinness. Recent studies have shown that 60 percent of girls aged ten to thirteen have dieted at least once. The emphasis on weight has created a monstrous situation with the result that one in one hundred teenagers suffers from anorexia nervosa; and bulimia is epidemic. After a twenty-year apprenticeship of going on diets, trying shots, pills, and fads, I discovered Overeaters Anonymous. I was desperate. It was a relief to hear that I had a disease and couldn't help myself. But I was told that I could arrest my disease one day at a time by following a twelve-step program. I decided that I had nothing to lose but my compulsion, so I stayed for eight years.

During those eight years I did not have one cookie, one scoop of ice cream, or one slice of cake!! I quit sweets cold turkey and adhered to the rigid low-carbohydrate eating plan that was given to me when I joined. Those years were full of pain and full of joy. By giving up my sugar "fix," I had nothing to turn to in order to put aside the stresses and anxieties of my life. I had to face my feelings for the first time and acknowledge my problems. I had to live life without a crutch of food—and it hurt.

To survive this ordeal, I had to learn how to cope with my problems and to change or resolve the issues that were most difficult to live with. In other words, I had to become an adult. The twelve steps of the Alcoholics Anonymous program adopted by OA taught me skills and problem-solving techniques. The only way to stay away from compulsive overeating was to practice the principles of this new program for living. It was like throwing a child who doesn't swim into the water. You either learn fast or sink.

Overeaters Anonymous is different from all other weight clubs in that it is more than a diet. The group borrowed the Alcoholics Anonymous program for recovery that maintains that compulsive eating is a threefold problem: physical, emotional, and spiritual. In all the years I attended OA, I saw many miraculous changes. They occurred when the individual did more than diet—when he or she lived the program for change.

I: Food Addiction: A Problem for Millions

Food abusers, like alcoholics, can be either "dry" or "sober." Being "dry" means that you are on a diet; you are imposing a temporary program for eating that will eliminate emotional binges as long as you stay "good." Being "dry" means that you are behaving a different way with food but are not doing anything to understand how your feelings or your life stresses contribute to compulsive overeating habits.

Sobriety is different. Being "sober" is a state of physical and emotional wellness. Sober people have given up binging and have learned or are learning to understand what issues in their lives cause them to eat (or drink). They then work to change these attitudes and unhappy situations.

One of the positive aspects of belonging to any weight club or support group is that you can get approval and love *right now*. You don't have to get thin or stay thin to be successful as a human being. After eight years in OA, I realized that I accepted all the members I met whether they were fat or thin. They didn't have to lose weight to please me. They were already lovable.

I saw that an important stumbling block for OA members was the belief that their problem was insoluble. As long as you believe that you are a victim of compulsive overeating, you are not in charge of your life. At any moment, the ax may fall and you go on a binge, not knowing why or how to stop.

After eight years in OA, I no longer believed I was powerless over food. I knew damned well I had the power, but I didn't know how to use it consistently. I decided to find another solution. I was tired of living my life being doomed to have an eating problem forever. I longed to be "normal."

After twenty years of diets and eight years of total abstinence from certain high-calorie foods, I was terrified at the thought that I could eat just one portion and stop. The belief that I was an all-or-nothing person who had no control over certain foods had been with me for a long time. I was doubtful that I, a college graduate with a master's degree, could ever be free of my obsession with food.

Looking back at those years when going without ice cream and dessert was no struggle, I tried to find out how I was able to maintain the restricted food intake so easily. I decided that during my years of participation in OA, all my needs were met. I received the love, approval, and help from my fellow members that I hadn't received in my life up until then but had yearned for. I had friends on call day and night. I didn't need food to take the place of loving feelings because I was getting the "real thing."

I discovered that to eliminate compulsive overeating, the problem eater must live a life of fulfillment. That means finding out which of her needs aren't being met and either getting them met or changing the situation and finding a better life. It means finding a specific lifestyle of consciousness, courage, and willingness to go forward, no matter what is necessary. The food addict must exchange martyrdom, victimhood, and pain for autonomy and power. I decided to share my experience with others, and I began by teaching classes based on the idea that self-esteem was the key to creating a better life. If a person felt good about herself and her life was happier, she would be more motivated to diet and be less inclined to eat because of stressful experiences.

Then I came across a concept that seemed to explain why so many diets had failed for so many people. Elizabeth Keyes in her book *How to Win the Losing Fight* put forth an idea called the "art of gentle eating." It was a precursor to behavior modification and was designed to help the binge eater learn to stop being afraid of food, stop depriving herself of favorite foods, and become responsible for eating what she wanted and stopping when satisfied. Along with this eating program was a set of ideas and meditations to increase self-acceptance and raise self-esteem.

Elizabeth Keyes's ideas encouraged me to teach people how to be free of the bondage of food. After all, the problem is not in the food but in the overeater. The more the food abuser blames food, the more she relinquishes her power to change her life. Although this program was exciting and offered a life free of dieting, I was amazed at how resistant people were to incorporate these concepts into their lives. How wonderful it would be to give up dieting forever! Why wasn't it easy to do?

Women who suffer from eating disorders are dedicated to the idea that the goal is to have a perfect body as soon as possible. The body must be pummeled, prodded, punished, and denied to give it the correct appearance. To seek freedom from compulsion is too long a process for most people. It takes hard work; you must look into yourself, and you must change. Very few people want to do that. They prefer the fantasy of a temporary diet that promises they will live happily ever after.

The nondiet approach was very popular and attracted many people. My students lost weight and seemed to enjoy the process. I evolved a system called "integral behavior modification" that went beyond the "art of gentle eating." I became aware of the ways compulsive eaters stopped themselves from reaching their goal. I called the point at which a dieter stops working and starts to regain her weight the "resistance point." I knew all the rationalizations for eating and cheating. Now I wanted to understand *why* so many women had to sabotage themselves at the "resistance point."

Some people stopped themselves halfway to their goal; others ran out of steam five pounds from success. Many binge eaters have a "magic number," a weight they never seem to go below. Each time they reach the "magic number," the diet goes out the window and they return to compulsive overeating and regain all the pounds they have lost. One day it dawned on me that the magic number symbolized the demarcation line between maintaining the status quo and the need for dramatic change in a person's life. The "magic number" is a fantasy. The dieter believes that something major will have to change in her life if she achieves her goal. That something may be overcoming fears of intimacy with men, talking back to an authority figure, quitting a job, disagreeing with a significant other, or getting a divorce. When you go below the "magic number," you have permission to be or do what you have wished but feared to do. Often the fear wins out, and the binger retreats to a safer place. The "resistance point" is the place at which fear surfaces.

Many dieters work hard to lose weight but know ahead of time at what weight they will run into trouble. I remember a young woman who had a paralyzing fear that something terrible might happen to her father. She feared that if she lost weight, she would become attractive to men and have to marry. Then she would have to leave home and would be unavailable if her father got sick or had an accident.

Another overweight woman kept herself from achieving her goal because she believed that she would have to confront her husband and ask for improvement in their relationship. She felt inadequate as an overweight person and thought she couldn't get anyone better. As long as she was too heavy, it was fine for her to settle for less. But if she looked prettier, she would have the right to a more satisfying marriage. If she demanded more, her husband might leave. She was more afraid of being alone than she was brave, so she stayed fat to avoid putting her self-worth to the test.

My private practice as a psychotherapist grew as I helped women work to learn what fat symbolized in their lives. Fat was not the problem, but it was a good cover-up for the real issues of fear of loss of love, relationship problems, guilt, poor self-concept, and nonassertiveness. And I found that although most overeaters wanted desperately to overcome the food compulsion, they really didn't want to change. The idea of things being different, of having to learn to ask for what they wanted, of having to go to work and support themselves, of moving away from the dependence on parents or spouse was too frightening for many.

In 1978 I wrote *How to Stop Playing the Weighting Game*, a workbook designed to help dieters and compulsive overeaters stop dieting and be free of their obsession with food. By doing the mental exercises and writing assignments in the book, the individual could learn to understand her beliefs about food, to recognize how and why she sabotaged attempts to lose weight or control overeating, and to practice techniques for behavioral change.

I wasn't the only one working to make sense of the dynamics of overeating and starvation in women. Therapist Susie Orbach in *Fat Is a Feminist Issue*, Kim Chernin in *Obsession: Reflections on the Tyranny of Slenderness*, and sociologist Jeanette Kupfermann in *The MsTaken Body* were professionals who wrote about the underlying issues of eating disorders. They pointed out that food and fat are not the primary problem. For some people, overeating is a problem-solving device. Diet removes fat but doesn't deal with the roots of the problem.

Throughout the years, many extremely thin women who said that they wanted to lose weight or learn to control their eating habits have joined my groups and classes. Although they were thin, they continued to talk about how inadequate they felt. The women who had fifty pounds to lose looked at the slim overeaters with amazement. These small women seemed to have achieved all that the obese women wanted, and yet they continued to speak of their misery. The fat women couldn't understand that happiness is an inside job. The thin women often felt misunderstood and ashamed that they looked thin, so frequently they dropped out.

Although I was teaching classes that were supposed to help people lose weight, I was really teaching classes in self-acceptance and consciousness-raising. My work has been a joy to me because I meet thousands of intelligent, creative, sensitive, responsive, lovable people . . . who don't know that is the truth about themselves. My job is to know that truth and to realize that eating disorders are not diseases in the physical sense. They are problem behaviors caused by false beliefs masquerading as truth.

Each person who comes to me has locked herself away in a prison of doubt, fear, and low self-worth. It is a prison without a lock on the door, but she doesn't realize that. She is locked in because she doesn't see any way out of the situations that she created for herself. My job is to help those suffering from eating problems "get out of jail."

Because compulsive eaters are so self-critical, the most important aspect of my work has been to create an attitude of change through love—not through punishment. If a person suffers from allergies, she is not considered a bad person for reacting to substances that are toxic to her body. An overeater is also reacting to toxic substances—toxic ideas and toxic situations. Her reaction to a poisonous emotional environment is to break out in a binge. My challenge is to get food abusers to see themselves in a new light so they can begin allowing themselves room for gradual change. Human development is two steps forward and one step back. We all learn from our mistakes. Food abusers want to be perfect *immediately* with no setbacks or slips. This is usually impossible to achieve. Baby steps are easier to handle.

Here is one way of looking at the progression from binge eater to healthy eater. I think that overcoming binge eating can be done in four developmental steps:

1. After the binge, you become aware of what triggered that binge.
2. In the midst of the binge, you become aware of the cause of the binge, but you keep eating.
3. Before you reach for the food, you are aware of why you are eating, but you go ahead and binge.
4. Before you reach for the food, you become aware of why you are eating, and you do something about the problem without eating.

The goal is consciousness. As long as you are on one of the four steps, you are becoming conscious of the dynamics of your behavior and are working toward a new alternative. When you finally reach step four, you may find that occasionally you revert to step one. That is human.

Another important premise in my work is the elimination of ideas like *good* and *bad* from the value system of my clients. As long as there is judgment, change is difficult to achieve. *Bad* simply means that you were anxious or stressed and did not have the resources to resolve the situation to your best advantage. *Good* means that you were conscious and making choices. One of my mottos is: "There is no good and no bad. There is only what you do and what you learn from that."

As long as the person suffering from an eating disorder hates her problem and hates herself for having it, she must punish herself. If she thinks of the eating disorder as an opportunity for growth, she will be able to learn how to deal with the world in such a way as to get the very best. I recently met a young woman who was recovering from anorexia nervosa. She told me that after many years of medical and psychological therapy, she had come to see that anorexia nervosa was a blessing in disguise. If she hadn't experienced this overwhelming problem, she would never have confronted her angers and fears about her family and her future. Recovering from anorexia meant that she had to learn to love herself and plan a happy and fulfilling life.

Eating disorders result when a minor difficulty is not handled correctly and continues until it becomes a problem. Every adolescent wrestles with the agonies of peer relationships, dating relationships, pressures at school, and family stresses that arise when he or she is starting to separate from the family and become a young adult. When the difficulty is mishandled so that the outcome is not a constructive solution, or when the unhealthy solution is applied over and over in the hopes that it will eventually work, the original difficulty becomes a serious problem. This is what happens with binge eating and with binge/purge behavior.

In the case of binge eating, a young woman may feel unhappy because she is dateless on Saturday night or doesn't feel accepted by peers. Her temporary solution may be to eat to soothe her unhappy feelings and to give herself a "feel good" to make up for the friendship she feels deprived of. At first, the food does seem to remove the misery. But, if each time this person feels left out she turns to food for comfort, she will soon find that her binges become obsessive. The binge takes over, and in addition to overcoming her relationship problems she has a new problem: compulsive overeating. The same is true of purging. As time goes on, the purger may find herself unable to stop the habit. Bulimia is the result.

1: I HAD TO WRITE THIS BOOK

I work to get the individual with an eating compulsion to risk giving up her old, ineffective solution to problem solving (abusing food) and learn a new approach. This book is the outgrowth of that work—devising strategies to help binge eaters find new ways to overcome their compulsive behaviors and find methods to face life and cope on a daily basis.

Twenty years ago, I was primarily concerned with the dynamics of dieting. During the last ten years, I have been treating many "thin fat" women, anorectics, and bulimics. These women have given up their autonomy over their bodies. They think they must diet because they tell themselves either they are too fat or that they are out of control with food and will become fat. To achieve a perfect body as portrayed by the media today, they starve themselves. Starvation leads to extreme hunger, which leads to uncontrolled eating. This cycle becomes a self-fulfilling prophecy and reinforces their fears and self-doubt about being acceptable and beautiful.

Working with the issues of women and their roles in a changing society has led me to offer classes and workshops in assertiveness training and new ways to recognize and deal with anger. As long as women choose to remain victims and believe that happiness comes from others, there will be eating disorders.

This book speaks mainly of women and their problems (and the majority of my clients are female), but there are an enormous number of males who are also compulsive overeaters. (A much small number of men are anorectic and bulimic.)

After teaching and counseling thousands of people who are obsessed with food, I have come to the conclusion that food abuse is a widespread social and cultural problem which we usually learn in the bosom of the family.

Food is easily available in this land of abundance. You will not be arrested for being drunk on food. It is not illegal to overeat. It is not as harmful as alcohol or drugs, although food abuse can lead to death when purging is practiced.

I had to write this book because I am sick and tired of reading about diets. Every month new books and magazine articles are written and sold that tell the individual how to lose weight. They reinforce how important it is to look good on the outside. I am tired of seeing beautiful young preteens and teenagers who tell me they are not good-looking enough to have a boyfriend or wear a bathing suit. They are curtailing their happiness and a chance for a fulfilling life even before it gets started.

I had to write this book to tell of the pain and suffering that comes from the irrational belief that how you look is more important than who you are. It is time we saw compulsive overeating as a universal sign of anxiety and stress that is not dealt with in a sane and productive way.

I had to write this book to encourage all persons with eating disorders to begin to see that they are not crazy and horrible people but wonderful people who need to learn new skills to have a life of joy.

People demand magic, a quick cure. There is no quick cure for eating disorders. A binger may be able to eliminate the symptom in a week or a month, but to achieve permanent freedom from addictive eating, she must be ready to spend a lifetime being self-aware and committed to face each situation that comes along and deal with it in a new way—without food. Once you have given up addictive eating, you must learn to live with your eyes open. Give up denying your negative feelings. Begin to ask for what you want. Value yourself so that you really believe that less than the best is unthinkable for you. It is a difficult job, but it is extremely rewarding. The results are happiness and a sense of mastery over your life.

YOU DESERVE THE VERY BEST!

CAUSES OF
ADDICTIVE EATING

Millions of people in our society use or abuse food the way an alcoholic abuses liquor. This is addictive eating, and it is a major aspect of most eating disorders. The three most recognized eating problems are anorexia nervosa, bulimia, and compulsive overeating. These are not diseases but groups of behaviors called syndromes, and are the result of biological, psychological, and sociological factors. Compulsive urges to overeat or gorge and purge may arise as a backlash to strict dieting or fasting, but it is also the inadequate coping mechanism of many people whose lives are filled with stress and loneliness.

What is compulsion? How is it possible to understand this kind of behavior? Why do so many people feel like slaves to these bad habits, obsessing about what to eat, or how to prevent themselves from binging or purging? Compulsion is loss of control and continuation of the behavior despite harmful consequences. In other words, if you cannot control when you start or stop an activity you have a problem!

John Bradshaw, well known authority on addictive behaviors, defines compulsion as "a mood altering event, experience, or thing, which brings major life problems." Both binging and starving change brain chemistry. We all are familiar with the use of fasting during religious rituals and retreats to create changes in consciousness. People with eating disorders are using pleasurable substances or behaviors to mask the pain of their lives. Gorging, purging and fasting are distractions from their real feelings. The obsession with food, weight, or exercise is a detour from feeling pain, anger, fear, and depression.

DON'T WORRY, BE HAPPY

Human beings have an innate aversion to physical or emotional pain. If we cannot avoid it, we will discover ways to lessen the discomfort. Society encourages us to use pleasure to mask pain or postpone the experience of anxiety, frustration or discomfort. Our national motto might well be: DON'T WORRY . . . BE HAPPY. As a result we encourage each other to eat, drink, spend, be sexual, get high, or escape. We believe in immediate relief and gratification. If one is good, more is better. Habits most associated with either strong feelings of pleasure or avoidance of distress are the most likely to develop into compulsions. Food is one of the most easily available and universally used substances which is abused.

Eating disorders arise when you learn to apply comforting activities involving food as solutions to life's problems, just as you apply a Band-Aid to a cut. But it is as if a person with an ulcer took an antacid; there is temporary relief, but the underlying condition remains and continues to flare up. By applying the same unsuccessful remedy of food as a temporary comfort over and over again, a new problem arises. The pleasurable act takes on a life of its own. The original situation which caused anxiety or discomfort is still there and now there is a new worry—addictive eating or starving.

Society tends to accept the abnormal as normal when it is common. We use phrases like "everyone is doing it" to absolve ourselves from guilt. We elect politicians or put our trust in religious leaders who tell us that they are upstanding citizens, and although we find out they are deceitful, dishonest, and often addicted to alcohol, drugs, and sex, we reelect them or continue to support their ministries.

How do we come to terms with these mixed messages? We learn to live in a state of denial. We tune out; we turn away; we avoid. Finally we forget, and forget we have forgotten.

During a televised sports show on a major network there was a public service announcement showing a well known basketball star, Magic Johnson, telling viewers to "just say NO to drugs." This was immediately followed by a commercial for beer. Most people watching probably didn't notice the hypocrisy of the message. We were being told that although dangerous drugs are rampant in this country, beer doesn't count. "Crazy-making" messages that encourage us to eat, drink and indulge but to stay thin in order to be loved or accepted are a major cause of eating disorders.

ADDICTION TO FEELINGS

Researchers Harvey Milkman and Stanley Sunderwirth believe that human beings crave three kinds of feelings: (1) relaxation, (2) excitement, and (3) fantasy or oblivion. Each of us seems to enjoy one of these sensations more than the others, sometimes to such a degree we create various ways to produce this feeling in order to replace discomfort or anxiety in our lives.

If you pleasure yourself by means of carbohydrate snacking, reading, TV watching, or using tranquilizers, you prefer a mellow, relaxed state for yourself. You may wonder at the people who adore roller coasters and thrills. These people enjoy feeling aroused or excited. They may find themselves drawn to sky diving, race car driving, compulsive spending, caffeine, cocaine, or gambling, while another segment of the population enjoys feeling oblivious to their surroundings and problems and may become addicted to anesthetic or psychedelic drugs. Meditation is a wonderful tool for achieving a state of altered consciousness in which you reach another plane of awareness, but some people don't know how to create the experience in a healthy way.

The theory that we tend to become addicted to feelings rather than substances, explains why all the people I have treated for eating disorders suffer from more than one compulsive problem. Many of the bulimic women in their twenties and thirties who have come to me report that

rs or sober alcoholics. They have
ion for another. They often abuse
spending as well. The majority of
rs seek relaxation or oblivion. Eating
ugary foods will produce a state of
y. The opposite is true for hypoglyce-
get "high" from sugar.

...at I called a "triple threat" client. She
was addi...   ugs, alcohol, and compulsive overeating.
Virginia told me her goal was to "not be." She craved the
oblivion of unconsciousness to avoid the pain of a childhood of physical and emotional abuse. The most efficient
way to accomplish this was by abusing drugs. When drugs
weren't available, she would drink until she passed out.
People like Virginia who want to avoid feelings and
problems, also escape into sleep. Another method of
achieving oblivion with drugs is to take flight into fantasy
through compulsive reading or computer games. Computer
hacks become so immersed in their fantasy world they
don't hear anything going on around them and can sit at
a computer terminal through the night.

BRAIN CHEMISTRY IS A MAJOR FACTOR

According to Drs. Milkman and Sunderwirth, adult
compulsions result from a combination of traumatic
childhood experiences, a genetic predisposition toward
compulsivity, and negative environmental pressures. They
have discovered that the reason some people prefer
relaxation while others crave excitement or fantasy is
differences in our brain chemistry.

I: Food Addiction: A Problem for Millions

Scientists now know that electrical activity in certain areas of the brain is responsible for experiences of pleasure and pain. Addictive behaviors result from self-induced changes in brain neurotransmitters. Compulsive individuals repeat specific behaviors to bring about activity in the brain nerve cells which create intense feelings. Different behaviors or substances lead to different sensations. Some people demonstrate in early childhood that they possess a subtle characteristic or genetic predisposition which steers them in the direction of addictive preferences.

A chemical called *serotonin* is synthesized in the brain and plays an important role in mood changes. Studies comparing the brain chemistry of people who died of natural causes with those who committed suicide show that those who took their own lives had much lower levels of serotonin. Lack of serotonin can affect your mood, producing irritability. An outstanding researcher in this field is Professor Richard Wurtman who has shown that serotonin is one of a number of brain chemicals affected by nutrients. Serotonin levels can be increased when a person consumes carbohydrates.

Doris, a bulimic, no longer used alcohol or drugs to dull her pain when she was unhappy and wanted to become oblivious to her surroundings and her feelings. She discovered that if she drank a quart of milk, she could escape into sleep. Milk contains *tryptophan*, an amino acid important in the manufacturing of serotonin.

Dr. Wurtman studied a group of obese students who were depressed and craved carbohydrates. He believed they had low serotonin levels and, although they were snacking on carbohydrates, their bodies were not produc-

24

ing a high enough level of serotonin to lift their depression. The students received a drug called *fenfluramine*, which increases serotonin levels. As a result, they significantly reduced their compulsive eating, and they felt less depressed.

THE CARBOHYDRATE FACTOR

Doctors Janice Keller Phelps and Alan Nourse, in their book *The Hidden Addiction and How to Get Free*, write that people who act compulsively or are addicted to substances are using these behaviors to get relief from depression. Continuous use of the substance or behavior wards off withdrawal or depressed feelings. They believe addiction arises from physiological or metabolic flaws in biochemistry which are usually genetic. Something may be wrong with the way the body of an addictive person handles sugar.

At times it is difficult to differentiate between the depression that results from biochemical imbalance and depression that results from the abuse of sugar, binge/purge behavior or starvation. Does the abuse of food create the depression or does the food addict use these behaviors as self-medication for an existing state of depression? Perhaps both are true.

FOOD AND THE FAMILY

Although researchers are discovering how important the physiology of the mind-body connection is in understanding eating disorders, a predisposition toward compulsivity does not guarantee that a person will definitely suffer from an eating disorder or addiction problem. One of the most important factors that interacts with biology and environment is childhood experience.

There are four types of family systems which are dysfunctional. If you are the product of one of these family types, you may still be suffering from the damage of your unhappy upbringing. They are: (1) Overachieving, (2) Judgmental, (3) Enmeshed, and (4) Distant. Your family may have combined attributes of more than one of these types. The result of growing up in one of these families is that you don't learn how to solve problems effectively, don't see how healthy people relate to each other, and may not have received adequate nurturing and acceptance. Therefore, you have formed a false self based on your unfortunate experiences.

PRESSURE TO ACHIEVE

The overachieving family strives for perfection. John Bradshaw often remarks in his workshop that some people grow up to become "human doings" instead of "human beings." The overachieving family pressures the child to achieve success. Each family defines success in a different way. In Maureen's family, success for women meant to be married to a successful man who made lots of money, while in Zoe's home, success meant being a college graduate. Barbie came from a family where the women were known for their looks and had won beauty contests or were professional models. Barbie had been a chubby child, and although, as an adult, she was tall and beautiful, her preoccupation with food and dieting in order to be thin enough to model and follow in her family's footsteps resulted in bulimia.

The commands of the overachieving family are often perfectionistic. A majority of young women with eating disorders have been told, "Make us proud of you!" Along with this is the demand to be a "good" child. What does a good child do? The child is supposed to already know the rules for being good, since they are seldom spelled out for her. These "good" girls have decided that they cannot let the family down. They must get excellent grades, never give their parents anything to worry about, never hurt anyone's feelings, and, of course, never get angry. They live by the belief, "what other people think is the most important thing." Appearances matter greatly. The pressure to achieve and look good at all costs made Kerry, an "A" student, cheat in high school in order to always come out on top.

The result of growing up in an overachieving family is the tendency to be highly self-critical and condemn yourself if you do not live up to the impossible standards you set. You don't realize that your expectations are irrational and unreachable because you are a result of your upbringing, and the environment of your dysfunctional family was the only model of the world you had. As a result you may be unable to give yourself credit for many of the wonderful talents and traits you already possess because you aren't perfect (thin enough) yet.

NEVER GOOD ENOUGH

The judgmental family is one where everyone hears what's wrong with them, but rarely is told what is right with them. Judgmental parents often abuse their children physically or verbally. Discount and ridicule make the child feel small and helpless. No matter what she does it won't be enough. She can't get her needs met, no matter how hard she tries. Some of these unhappy children decide that they'll never be good enough and grow up settling for mediocre lives of quiet desperation. Others build a wall between themselves and other people. They are afraid to trust, so they become extremely independent and appear confident and successful, yet they constantly battle their inner guilt and shame which they cannot share with another soul.

In the unhappy setting of the judgmental family the commands are: "Don't do as I do, do what you're told," "Don't ask questions," and "Don't feel your feelings." The controlling family doesn't allow you to be you because the you that you are is not what pleases them. One common misconception is that feeling sad or crying is a sign of weakness, so don't have these feelings. Anger is a "no-no." Judgmental parents say things like, "There's nothing to be scared of," "There's nothing to be mad at," "Why do you want to feel like that?"

Since you aren't allowed to feel what you feel, where do the feelings go? You bury them. Some people learn to eat to stuff them down. Anorexics numb their rage and despair through starvation. In their minds, to eat is to feel. Without anger you turn into a "people pleaser." Many obese overeaters use their fat as a protection or armor against the judgment and shame created in the family.

28

Adults who grew up in judgmental families have very low self-esteem. These women often seek relationships with judgmental men or become co-dependents in relationships with other addictive people.

WHOSE LIFE IS IT?

The enmeshed family is a clinging family. "All for one and one for all" could be its motto. An outsider looking at an enmeshed group may think they are one big happy family, but they aren't. Each member is a slave to the idea that it is "us against them," or "united we stand, divided we fall." Loretta's family brainwashed her to believe, "we are the only ones you can really trust. We'll always be here for you. There's no place like home." Yet each time that Loretta tried to find comfort and acceptance in the bosom of her family, she was verbally abused or discounted. Her father was usually unavailable because he was a work-aholic. Her mother, a compulsive overeater and gambler, was either away playing cards or acted critical and angry. Love came in the form of food or money.

Members of the enmeshed family have no lives of their own. Privacy is not honored. John Bradshaw describes it like being in a room with the doorknob on the outside. Anyone can enter anytime, and there's nothing you can do about it. In a healthy family, it is like being in a room with the doorknob on the inside. You have control over your privacy and the degree of intimacy you allow. Clinging families believe that your business is everybody's business. Boundaries are gone. There are no secrets. Nothing can be withheld.

You don't get to have your own life in an enmeshed family. Instead, you may grow up believing that you are responsible for other people's happiness. Almost every person suffering from food addiction is trying to make mother or father feel good. John was 50 years old and still called his mother every day, like a dutiful child. Molly's elderly parents called Molly to solve their problems and mediate their fights. She had to drive one hour each way to their home, never hesitating when the call came. Although she was acting like a "loving" daughter, Molly had to lose work time, and she neglected her husband and child while catering to her parents. People in enmeshed families never truly feel strong and independent. They may look grown-up and be geographically separate, but they are still bound by an umbilical cord of guilt and shame to their family.

STAY COOL

The distant family may also be an overachieving or a judgmental family. The hallmark of this system is a lack of emotional involvement. People don't act loving. They may be both physically undemonstrative, rarely hugging, kissing, or touching, and they may also refrain from verbal expressions of warmth and support.

When Lydia brought home "A's" on her report card her mother rarely praised her. So Lydia tried even harder to get a response. She graduated at the top of her high school class and was accepted by a prestigious college where she did outstanding work. Then she went on to an illustrious career. Lydia knew that her mother bragged about her daughter to her friends and neighbors, but Lydia never heard it. By this time Lydia was both an overachiever and overeater. How much would she have to do, how many honors would she have to earn in order to hear, "I love you?"

Bonnie came from an emotionally cool family too. Her family only hugged and kissed when people were getting on an airplane or arriving home from a trip. She was uncomfortable with physical touches yet yearned to be close to people. Bonnie developed a way of hiding her shyness by holding herself aloof. The other children in her neighborhood thought she was stuck up, but she was only hiding her fear of rejection. She spent many hours alone, fantasizing and eating.

Distant families avoid emotion. They may not express anger openly or talk about their feelings. They just go through the motions of living. Again, to the casual observer, they may appear as perfect as an episode of "Father Knows Best." On the surface everything looks wonderful and happy, but underneath the calm surface, the family members are in great pain because there is no intimacy.

Growing up in an inadequate family environment doesn't prepare you for dealing with life. When you find yourself in a high risk situation or relationship you may be overwhelmed by feelings of pain or helplessness. Food abusers automatically turn to binging or starving in order to turn off their feelings and become numb. Many sufferers of eating disorders come from families where there is a history of alcohol, drug or food abuse or indicators of familial depression. The combination of: (1) a biological predisposition toward addiction, (2) an unhappy family history, and (3) a society which encourages us to feel good at any cost leads inevitably to compulsive and addictive behaviors.

3

WHO BINGE EATS?

Ingesting large quantities of food in short periods of time can become an addiction. The binge behavior then takes on a life of its own, and the problem eater is hooked into a vicious cycle of feast or famine. Surprisingly, the central issue is not food, although the sufferer spends a tremendous amount of time worrying about and discussing food and body weight. The issues underlying eating disorders are directly related to problems such as low self-esteem, perfectionism, rejection, loneliness, and control over one's life.

These same concerns affect the lives of many people who do not turn to food. Millions of people have come from broken homes or have parents who are alcoholics, abusive, or absent. Many men and women suffer from the need for approval and fear of rejection. Not all of these people turn to food as a solution. Each person who has experienced fear, guilt, anxiety, stress, or pain has developed his or her own particular ways of coping. Some people drink, others use drugs, smoke, or get lost in overwork, compulsive sexual activity, sleep, and even chronic illnesses such as headaches, stomachaches, or backaches. Millions choose food as a tranquilizer. A few tackle their problems head-on and learn to resolve them and to deal directly with emotional pain.

Your choice of coping mechanism can be linked to the problem feelings you are trying to deal with. Alcohol seems to be the choice for many who want to reduce anxiety and depression or cope with loneliness or feelings of inadequacy. It seems to release inhibitions and emotions. Nicotine reduces awareness of tension. Workaholism may make you feel better about yourself because you may gain praise from others and feel in control. Getting lost in work also helps you avoid the stress of intimate relationships. Compulsive sexual activity may temporarily reduce the sense of isolation and give you a sense of power or control. Food also reduces tension and relieves anxiety and depression. For some binge eaters, the abuse of food promotes withdrawal from intimate or sexual experiences.

These actions serve different purposes. For one group of individuals, abusing substances or engaging in compulsive acts are the only way they have learned to, or believe they can, deal with their emotional lives. Overdoing alcohol, drugs, food, and so on may be a method of suppressing or denying positive or negative feelings or both. Many food abusers actually can't stand happiness and overeat to "suppress the sublime"! Some, who are relatively happy, eat as "insurance" to reinforce good feelings and distance themselves from the possibility of unhappiness.

These attempts to reduce stress and eliminate pain may be inappropriate and harmful for the realistic resolution of the problem, but they are temporarily soothing and pleasurable. Binge eating does not solve the problems, but it numbs the eater so she thinks her worries are over for the time being. Binge eating becomes an addictive process in which the binger uses excessive pleasure to erase pain.

TYPES OF BINGE EATERS

We can identify three kinds of people in the world: True-thins, Thin-fats (a term coined by Dr. Hilde Bruch), and Fat-fats. True-thins are people who never worry about their weight or what they eat. They eat when they are hungry and that's that! They are not slaves to the scale because they know that their bodies will not betray them but will digest and assimilate what they eat as nature decreed.

Thin-fats are people, both men and women, who are obsessed with the fear of getting fat. Those who fast and starve to reach an impossible goal of skeletal thinness are called anorectics. The people who are terrified of becoming fat but will not starve, alternately binge by eating huge quantities of food and then purge by vomiting or ingesting large amounts of laxatives or diuretics. We call these people bulimics.

Fat-fats are overweight or even morbidly obese individuals who are also driven to swings of dieting and binging, but they do not purge. In this book, I call them compulsive overeaters. Their binges result in weight gains that drive them to renew their attempts to diet again and again.

The popularity of organizations like Weight Watchers and Overeaters Anonymous, and the overwhelming success of diet books, are testimony to the numbers of people who are concerned with the questions of weight reduction. The National Association of Anorexia Nervosa and Associated Disorders estimates that there are five hundred thousand bulimics in the United States. I think this is an extremely conservative estimate. The response to a survey by *Glamour* magazine proved that eating disorders are reaching worldwide proportions. In a 1981 survey of college students, 13 percent of the normal college population experienced all of the major symptoms of bulimia; 87 percent of this group were women.

The definition of beauty has changed dramatically in the past thirty years; now curves are "out," and a boyish, tubular look is "in," which puts a lot of pressure on women (and some men). To look like an adolescent boy, most women have to spend inordinate amounts of time dieting and focusing on their bodies. Thin-fats as well as Fat-fats spend billions of dollars to strip away fat through spas, diet centers, nutritional counseling, gyms, medical regimens, and diet clubs.

Anorexia nervosa, bulimia, and compulsive overeating are part of a spectrum of eating disorders that embrace a wide range of behaviors, some of which fall in between these three categories.

The American Psychiatric Association classifies only anorexia nervosa and bulimia as eating disorders. I believe that compulsive overeating, leading to obesity, is also an eating disorder. Not officially classed as a psychiatric problem, compulsive overeating involves behavior and underlying causes similar to those attributed to anorexia and bulimia. It is time that people recognized that binge eating is not just a bad habit but a major psychological disorder of overweight people as well as starvers.

The abuses of food as they are described below seem at first to resolve inner pressure, but as the act of fasting and/or binging becomes more and more important, the abuser realizes that food is no longer the answer but has become a problem in itself. This realization causes increased anxiety, because the answer is no longer as pleasurable as before. It no longer helps the person cope efficiently and causes symptoms that produce new problems. The attempted cure becomes the disease.

ANOREXIA NERVOSA

Eating disorders do not "just happen" to an individual. He or she is always a very active participant in the process. Anorexia nervosa is voluntary self-starvation to the point of losing 15 percent of body weight, which sometimes leads to death. Anorectics seem to have formidable self-control, determination, and willpower; they follow incredibly punishing exercise regimens or deny themselves nourishment. Yet in the midst of their starvation, they are obsessed with thoughts of food. Many anorectics collect cookbooks and do the cooking for others while ignoring their own hunger.

Dramatic weight loss plus loss of menstrual periods are the major criteria for diagnosis of anorexia nervosa. In addition, anorectics may suffer from a general slowing down of the metabolism. Hair becomes limp, fingernails become brittle, pulse rate falls, and the individual complains of being cold all the time. The body begins to feed upon itself, and the anorectic becomes progressively weaker although she may continue pushing herself to exercise to burn off calories.

Anorectics differ from bulimics and compulsive overeaters in that self-starvation leads to mental and emotional deterioration, so that she no longer thinks clearly or perceives reality in a normal way. Deep depression is a common state of mind. As she loses touch with reality, she continues to maintain that she is fat.

Anorexia must be treated both medically and psychologically. Medical intervention is mandatory to bring the anorectic's body back to health and proper functioning. Psychological counseling deals with obsessional thinking and behavioral retraining.

The American Psychiatric Association has classified anorexia nervosa as an unremitting course that progresses to death. Anorexia usually begins in adolescence, and 95 percent of its sufferers are females, as opposed to 5 percent males. Here are the main features of anorexia:

- Intense fear of becoming fat
- Distorted body image: claiming to be fat even when emaciated
- Weight loss of at least 15 percent of original body weight
- Refusal to maintain a minimal normal weight
- No physical illness that would cause extreme weight loss

There are two types of anorectics: restrictors and bulimics. A restrictor is a person who diets or fasts to lose weight by reducing total intake, especially cutting out foods high in carbohydrates and fats. Bulimic anorectics starve but also alternate periods of binging and purging. Bulimic anorectics are playing a dangerous game because purging can alter the body chemistry. Chemical or fluid imbalance can lead to cardiac arrest and death.

Although anorexia has been seen primarily in middle- and upper-middle-class Caucasian girls between the ages of twelve and twenty-five, this condition is becoming more and more widespread in industrialized countries.

The key issue for anorectics, bulimics, and compulsive overeaters is control or power. Anorectics tend to be obedient, high-achieving, "good" boys and girls. They do not rebel but tend to be overly compliant and sweet. During adolescence, the time a young person begins to ask, "Who am I?" the youngster tells herself that she has no impact on her world. She can, however, control her own body. Limiting her food intake and engaging in extremes of physical exercise give her a feeling of power. Refusing food can also be seen as an act of rebellion against the control of parents.

The changes that puberty brings—growth spurts, additional body fat, sexual maturation—seem undesirable to the anorectic girl. She views her body as ugly and deformed. She begins to believe that a thin body is both desirable and powerful. And she decides that her mind must subdue her body to prove her autonomy.

Another way of expressing her determination is through compulsive exercise. There is an ascetic quality about the way that anorectics punish their bodies. One unique quality in anorectics who compulsively exercise is their avoidance of passive or receptive pleasures. Compulsive overeaters and bulimics fight against the episodic "indulgence" of overdoing food, sex, or spending. Anorectics, however, seem unable to allow themselves pleasure in any form. They usually feel empty, hungry, tired, and in pain. They seem to feel great joy in maintaining this state of deprivation because they focus on the sense of power that comes from mastery over the body while they ignore the pain.

Many young girls become preoccupied with dieting yet do not become anorectic. Anorexia may result from the interaction of excessive dieting with other factors, such as the search for identity, struggle for control over one's life, self-worth, and family relationships. There may even be a biological predisposition that triggers anorexia when emotional stress becomes overwhelming.

Anorexia has been viewed as an attempt to make time stand still. The anorectic, by interrupting her physical development through starvation, stays the size of a child with the asexual characteristics of a child. She may be afraid of adult responsibilities and changes that she fears she cannot handle. Most anorectics are involved with their families in ways that keep them from achieving a sense of independence.

One common feature of the anorectic personality is the feeling of being responsible for making someone else (usually the parent) feel good. Anorectics are constantly trying to second-guess others, read their parents' minds, and to live up to their fantasized dream of what their parents expect from them. The anorectic can be compared to a clean slate upon which others write. She will be or do what they want her to be or do. The parents of this wonderful child do not realize that the lack of rebellion and the overly good-girl behavior is abnormal. The family is not aware that beneath the exterior of the people-pleasing, overachieving, seemingly happy child is a person who lacks self-esteem and feels powerless. It is only through acting out the eating disorder that the girl finally makes the statement of her pain and frustration.

Perfectionism plagues anorectics. Somehow the individual decides that thin is perfect; therefore, she is not perfect until she is thin enough. I once asked an anorectic woman what her goal was. She replied, "I will be perfect when I can exist on zero calories." Another said, "If I'm not ninety pounds I might as well be two hundred pounds." Often, the anorectic comes from a family in which appearances, physical attractiveness, and respect by the community (the "what will people think?" attitude) were stressed. Conflict results when the young person is caught between the drive for perfection and the constant feeling that she is not good enough and never will be.

Anorexia seems to involve younger adolescents and bulimia young adults. It may be that the emotional upheavals of separating from the family, which take place in the late teens and early twenties, are a factor in the onset of the latter eating disorder. Perhaps the young adult is eager to be on her own but experiences fear and uncertainty about herself as an individual and as a strong person. Ties to her family, both happy and unhappy, can lead to feelings of guilt either for running away or for not staying to take care of others.

The longer the anorectic ignores her symptoms or denies that she has a problem, the longer it will take to regain a normal life. Some anorectics die as a result of the physical damage that results from starvation. Many regain weight but continue to be obsessed with fear of getting fat and choose to become bulimic, having periods of binge eating and purging. Treatment may have to start with hospitalization to restore the body. Psychotherapy is a must, and treatment of the entire family should be encouraged to help the anorectic grown and understand herself so she can separate from her childhood and her family and take the next step into healthy adulthood.

BULIMIA

Bulimics are preoccupied with their weight and attempt to control it by dieting, fasting, vomiting, or purging with laxatives or diuretics. Conflicts about food and weight dominate their lives. The foods consumed during a binge often have high caloric content. They may be sweets high in carbohydrates, and they often have a texture that facilitates rapid eating and vomiting. Once the bulimic has begun a binge, she continues to crave more food. She feels out of control and is afraid she will not be able to stop.

Some of the characteristics of bulimic behavior are:

- Recurring binge episodes; eating a large amount of food in a short period of time
- Eating high-calorie foods
- Eating inconspicuously or secretly
- Ending the eating episode by self-induced purging
- Repeated attempts to lose weight through dieting, vomiting, and use of laxatives or diuretics

- Frequent weight fluctuations caused by alternating binges and fasts
- Feeling depressed and thinking hateful thoughts about oneself
- Intense fear of being of becoming fat
- Preoccupation with exercise

Bulimia often starts out as a way of "having your cake and eating it too." Many weight-conscious teenagers learn that they can overeat and stay slim by vomiting. This practice allows the girl to feel the pleasure of eating and avoid the consequences painlessly (at first). Many teens try this method but grow out of it or realize that it is harmful and stop. But some young women become hooked on the practice. Soon the pleasure diminishes and the act of purging seems to take on a life of its own. Finally, the act of binging and purging becomes the center of the bulimic's existence. It is her only coping mechanism and her only source of pleasure at the same time. And it has become a problem because she can't stop it even though she wishes to.

The bulimic knows that her eating patterns are abnormal and fears not being able to stop no matter how hard she tries. Yet she is afraid of giving up purging because of her intense fear of gaining weight. She sees only two alternatives: remain in the prison of binge/purge or be fat.

Bulimia is not a physical disorder. It is not a disease but a group of behaviors that become an obsession for the sufferer. Most bulimics are within a normal weight range; some may be underweight and some overweight. It has been suggested that as many as 60 percent of anorectics have bulimic episodes.

According to a survey conducted by UCLA, most bulimics have been overweight at some time. The average bulimic starts to diet at age fifteen and by age eighteen is in a state of chaos from her binging and fasting. By twenty-one she is into the full-blown binge/purge cycle. Forty percent of those replying to the UCLA survey also admitted to doing an illegal act such as shoplifting. This behavior pattern seems to be common to bulimics and anorectics. Compulsive overeaters also have often had a history of stealing small items such as food, clothing, or notions. Compulsive exercise regimens in which the person exercises without enjoyment or overdoes the amount and length of exercise time is another factor in both bulimic and anorectic behaviors.

Bulimia begins in adolescence when a young woman turns to dieting, at first for fun, but later comes to equate self-esteem with body image and attractiveness. Bulimia may continue for many years. I have worked with women who have had intermittent bulimic episodes for more than twenty-five years. Usually their binges alternate with periods of normal eating. The majority of bulimics are young adult women. I believe that their bulimia results from the conflict of modern woman trying to be all things to all people. In our culture, women are judged both at work and in their social lives by their beauty, whereas men gain respect largely through ability or power. There are some men, of course, many of them athletes, who must conform to certain weight standards. They become obsessed with the need to control their weight or their compulsion to overeat and do so through purging.

The majority of women with bulimia are "people-pleasers" who are unable to express negative feelings and also unable to ask for what they want. The self-hatred and torment of the woman who binges and purges leads her to live a double life, appearing slim and serene to the outside world but secretly living with her head in the toilet bowl much of the time, afraid of being found out.

One of the biggest handicaps for the bulimic is her extremely low self-esteem. Although the bulimics I have worked with are usually intelligent, creative achievers, they constantly denigrate themselves. Bulimics are driven by perfectionism, which produces helpless feelings and reinforces their sense of worthlessness. Such feelings provoke more eating. The binge/purge process is inflamed by self-hatred over lack of perfect control of food. All this proves that the victim is unworthy. It is a nightmarish cycle of self-judgment leading to eating as both a punishment and a relief from pain.

The bulimic is at the mercy of the self-critic in her thoughts, an unrelenting parental critique which insists that she is not and never will be OK. As a young adult woman she often wants to be involved in a love relationship. If she already has a negative view of herself as an undesirable love object, her constant exposure to the ads and magazine articles about health in which very thin models are shown as examples of physical beauty makes her assume that thin is perfect and fat equates to failure. No one will want her unless she is perfect/thin. Until then, she must be alone; but being alone is stressful. Loneliness leads to binge eating for comfort. This leads to more thoughts about being imperfect and "not ready yet." She can't be loved until she looks right, but she can't look right because she eats over lovelessness. Depression follows these thoughts, and it becomes increasingly harder for the binge eater to reach her goal.

Unlike anorectics, bulimics are sexually active women, some even promiscuous. Some desire acceptance and approval of the opposite sex to the point of undergoing cosmetic surgery to appear more alluring or more "perfect," hence lovable. Throughout all this, the bulimic is haunted by her fear that her terrible behavior will be discovered. Therefore, she often keeps an emotional distance from men. The desire for intimacy and fear of intimacy lead the bulimic to a stalemate. Some women date casually but back away from long-term relationships. Many who are married still maintain a wall of secrecy and pretend that things are fine when they are not. They feel isolated most of the time.

What differentiates the bulimic from other bingers is the purge. Purge behavior starts out as a simple method to avoid weight gain but comes to take on a life of its own. The act of purging may be symbolic, just as the binge behavior is. The bulimic is unwilling to assimilate her food just as she is unwilling to assimilate her feelings about her life problems. Bulimics have trouble committing themselves to a program for change because they are ambivalent about whether they actually want to confront their problems.

On one level, the bulimic considers her behavior a form of self-control. Whereas many people view vomiting as a sign of lack of control, she sees it as evidence that she is in command of her body; many bulimics can vomit just by thinking about it. Food is an intrusion which she has the power to ward off.

Conflict about getting over the problem arises from the distorted belief that if she gives up binging, she won't have enough food. She believes she will be stuck in a lifetime of permanent deprivation because to maintain a thin body, she will have to diet forever. The bulimic wants to overeat and be thin at the same time. She does not realize that it is possible to be thin and eat all kinds of food. She will only have to give up overeating, not healthy eating, but she hasn't learned to see that choice as an alternative because of her diet-conscious, deprived outlook.

Another reason the bulimic often hesitates to change her behavior is that bulimia is a detour on the road of life. She is able to avoid larger issues or questions about herself as a successful person as long as she is obsessed with the eating problem, which eclipses everything else: relationships, career, and health. The bulimic becomes so preoccupied with her destructive behavior that there is no time left for serious work or intimate relationships. If she gives up binging and purging, she will have to risk putting herself on the line to achieve her life goals. She may fail or she may succeed. Many people are just as afraid of success as they are of failure. Staying bulimic means never having to find out.

Purging may be thought of as a cleansing act. After gorging on thousands of calories of food, the binger is usually so uncomfortable that she wishes to get rid of the food as soon as possible. Some purgers have told me that cleansing the system was a way to eliminate guilt. One bulimic talked at length about her apartment being dirty even when she cleaned it. She felt that way about her body. When she put food into it, she dirtied the body. Ritual vomiting kept her clean and pure.

Bulimia differs from other types of overeating in that the binges are often violent episodes involving many thousands of calories. Vomiting cancels out the huge caloric debt she has incurred, but it also aggravates the problem, because by removing the penalty of weight gain, purging also removes the restraints on binging. Thus the episodes of overeating become more and more compelling in her life, and she feels increasingly isolated by her shameful secret.

There are different degrees of bulimic behavior. More is known about anorectics who binge than about bulimics who are, and have always maintained, a normal weight. The prognosis for normal weight bulimics is more positive than for those who have been or are anorectic.

Although eating disorders have not been studied extensively or over a long period of time, most bulimics who have been treated come from middle- to upper-middle-class families. These families have a higher than average incidence of alcoholism, depression, and weight problems.

COMPULSIVE OVEREATING

At the far end of the spectrum of eating disorders is compulsive overeating. The majority of compulsive eaters are overweight because they do not purge. Compulsive overeaters are both male and female and of all ages and classes. Some are periodic bingers, others binge daily. Some compulsive eaters do not have bouts of excessive gorging but eat continuously. It is as if an intravenous feeder is dripping nutrients into the body in a constant

48

flow to tranquilize and calm the underlying violent emotions. Compulsive overeaters share many characteristics of bulimia:

- Recurring binge episodes; eating large amounts of food in a short period of time
- Eating high-calorie food
- Sometimes eating secretly
- Repeated attempts to lose weight
- Frequent fluctuations of weight caused by alternating binges and fasts or diets
- Feeling depressed and thinking hateful thoughts about oneself

Bulimics fear getting fat while compulsive overeaters fear becoming thin (but don't always know it). Some obese overeaters use excess food intake as a way to deal with uncomfortable feelings, to soothe stress, and to relieve anxiety. Others eat to calm themselves but also to be fat. Fat acts as a protective covering for these people.

Some overweight individuals hang on to excess pounds as a health measure even in this age when we know that lean bodies are healthier. In the pre-penicillin age, many more children died than now. It was widely believed that if you were larger, you were healthier and could fight off disease and survive. Skinny children were fed cream, tonics, and rich foods to "put meat on their bones." To this day, some fat people fear that they will become ill if they get too thin.

A corollary of this myth is the fear of cancer. Sufferers of cancer lose weight quickly. Sometimes an obese client has shared a fear that if she loses weight "without trying" she may be ill and doesn't know it. "I'll just gain a few pounds back to ensure that I'm OK." Another fantasy fear that I have come across is the "holocaust fear." The overweight individual is worried about being lean because "What if it happened again? I couldn't survive in a concentration camp!"

In addition to fears about life and health, some compulsive overeaters hang on to fat as a way of denying sexuality, reflecting conflict about sex roles in society. Many overweight women avoid sex because they feel unworthy or ugly. They not only turn their partners away, they turn themselves off and stop feelings of arousal. Denying sexual feelings may resolve fears of being "bad" or promiscuous if they followed their natural impulses. Many fat people have told me that they are afraid that if they lost weight they might act out their sexual fantasies and bring shame upon themselves.

Fat resulting from binge eating may also be an expression of anger by many women toward men and society. Certain women who want to bow out of the race to be a sex object or a perfect "10" use fat as a cover-up. They are saying, "Look at the real me, not just the package." People with low self-esteem may feel uncomfortable when noticed by the opposite sex. Fat is a big coat that covers up and protects the person.

Most compulsive eaters seem to live from the neck up. The majority shy away from exercise. They are not in touch with their bodies. One woman told me that she lived in her brain, and her body was just the pedestal upon which her head rested. Compulsive overeaters live in a paradoxical state; they hate their bodies but are consumed with the need to control and shape up the very body they want to ignore. Whereas bulimics are exquisitely sensitive to every rumble and gurgle of their insides, compulsive eaters tend to be totally unaware of what is happening within. They tune out messages about hunger and satiety and eat mostly from emotional stimulation.

As in the case of anorectics and bulimics, compulsive eaters also have a need for approval which leads them to become compliant people-pleasers. Most overeaters give more than they receive from others. The jolly fat man is the stereotype of this group. Many female overeaters are the "Earth Mother" type, or what I call the "Statue of Liberty," saying "Give me your tired, your poor . . ."

A third reason for binging to get or remain fat may be to avoid dealing with another, more important problem. As long as the compulsive eater is trying to work on her weight, she has an excuse for not taking a look at her unhappy marriage, her inability to get a job in which she is respected and liked, or her inability to express anger. Both bulimics and compulsive eaters maintain their behaviors to skirt issues of success and failure.

Like bulimics, compulsive overeaters are often perfectionists who drive themselves to overachieve and then punish themselves for falling short. Unlike the bulimic, however, the overeater cannot hide her problem. Looking fat and feeling unacceptable because of it adds to the unhappiness and anxiety of the overeater the way secrecy adds to the stress of the bulimic.

I believe that anorexia nervosa, bulimia, and compulsive overeating are all different expressions of the same disorder. They are the food-related ways that some people have devised to try to solve their life problems. All food abusers are involved with the same issues: self-concept, control, social acceptance and approval, fear of rejection and abandonment, and the inability to express negative feelings in an appropriate way.

Each subtype of eating disorder arises from differences in the cultural background, family history, family eating habits, genetic predisposition, and personality development of the individual. Both medical and psychological factors play a part. Medical researchers are exploring the relationship between the chemistry of the brain and possible irregularities in the hypothalamus as factors that may be the reason for turning to dysfunctional food behaviors as a way of expressing conflicts instead of some other pathological behavior. I have observed the psychological factors, however, and I find that personal choice and behavior can be learned, *can be changed*, and that these changes will affect physical functions toward health and balance.

Anorectics, bulimics, and compulsive overeaters have all tried to resolve issues in slightly different ways. Anorectics try to control life by controlling their body and food intake until it becomes an obsession that leads to severe physical debilitation and even death. Bulimics stand a middle ground, alternately gorging and purging in their attempt to be OK in the world, and compulsive overeaters cope with life's problems by binging. None of these are practical or positive solutions. The only way out of the eating disorder is to learn new ways of being and new methods of surviving in the emotional jungle.

4

WHAT IS A BINGE ?

Like the word *love*, the word *binge* is bandied about and used to mean many things. Let's define it here and now. Binge eating is the one behavior that is common to anorexia nervosa, bulimia, and compulsive overeating. Binge eaters may be emaciated, normal weight, or fat. They are obsessed with planning binges, evaluating binges, and avoiding binges. The dictionary definition of the word *binge* is "a period of excessive indulgence; a spree." The word *indulge* implies giving in to a whim. In other words, you lack control over your behavior. This leads to the idea that what you are doing is bad.

At this time, there are no official criteria for defining a binge. Some health professionals would like to use the amount of calories consumed as a rule of thumb, with 2,000 calories being the low limit. One bulimic was reported to have consumed 50,000 calories during one binge episode. The nature of the binge is, therefore, important to understand because there is great variety in amounts of food or liquid ingested, time or duration of the binge, and emotional states experienced by the binge eater.

A binge is an episode of uncontrolled eating. I will not define it according to the number of calories ingested because I have spoken to people who feel anxious and filled with self-hatred after eating only six cookies. Their feelings are as strong as those of people who have downed six dozen cookies or twenty dollars' worth of food. I have read the food diaries of countless bingers over the years, and I have come to realize that most binge experiences share several common factors:

- Eating when not hungry
- Eating without enjoyment
- Guilt before, during, and/or after eating
- A sensation of a void that does not get filled no matter how much is eaten
- Frenzy: eating rapidly without tasting the food
- Eating a large amount
- Feeling out of control, unable to stop

Emotional energy characterizes the experience of a binge eater. It is as if the binge eater were caught up in a tidal wave that starts slowly and carries her along to a greater and greater feeling of frenzy and panic. She gets lost in the binge, finding a temporary respite from her emotional pain. One woman said that during her ten-year binge/purge experience she felt numb most of the time. Overeating tranquilizes the surge of emotions that the binger imagines are threatening to engulf her. The binge only postpones realization of the feeling until another, and possibly safer moment, usually after the threatening situation or event has passed.

Lori had a weekend of binge eating and purging. It started after she "had to" attend a picnic with her family. Since this was a yearly event, she knew ahead of time what to expect. She was afraid to go because she knew there would be a great array of attractive foods that she usually forbade herself. She knew that once she was there, her desire for the forbidden foods would overwhelm her self-discipline. But she ignored her feelings because she didn't want to disappoint her mother by not going. I asked her to rate the event on a scale of 1 to 10 according to the degree of discomfort and anxiety it caused her. She gave it a 9.

Since she would not give herself permission to avoid the picnic, she gave up control and gave in. She numbed herself with food for two reasons: to calm her feelings of unhappiness at being in an uncomfortable situation and because the temptation of fattening foods was overwhelming. Then she made herself throw up. Her subsequent binge/purge episodes (the next day) were caused by her disappointment with herself for losing control at the picnic. Anger at being a victim of circumstances and self-hatred at her behavior snowballed into a vicious cycle. Lori's coping behavior of vomiting to get rid of binge overload was as anxiety-producing as the situations she was trying to deal with and led to additional binging and purging.

A BINGE IS A TEMPER TANTRUM!

A binge always has to do with feelings——usually resentment, frustration, and rage. There are two kinds of temper tantrum binges: food anger and emotional anger.

Food anger is the sense of frustration experienced after long-term or constant dieting. The weeks or months of carefully following menus lead to a build-up of a feeling of deprivation. The dieter goes wild. She can't eat one scoop of ice cream but must consume a half gallon. One portion is never enough after such a long period of going without. It is as if the little child within is saying, "I'll show you. You can't take my goodies away. *I want it*!" Rose lost eighty pounds during a six-month fast. She has always liked bread best of all foods. After six months with no such food, she ate an entire package of six English muffins at a time——one would not fill the void.

Food anger also arises from the boomerang effect when fasting is used as a means of binge prevention. It is like holding your breath for as long as you can and then letting go. Many bulimics hold off eating a meal until mid-afternoon or eat only once a day. The build-up of deprivation can result in a binge meal rather than a moderate meal. This out-of-control experience is unpleasant. The bulimic then tells herself that eating is dangerous and must be avoided.

Anorectics, bulimics, and compulsive overeaters are always dieting. They keep themselves in a constant state of deprivation. When Joan's dates want to take her out for dinner, for example, she panics. She is terrified of eating and would prefer to fast or eat only salad, and she hopes to go as long as possible without having to make decisions about food. She often fills herself with tea or soda to quiet her raging stomach. She can follow this strict regimen for two or three weeks at a time before all her resolve disappears and she eats uncontrollably. After each debacle, she swears that she must stay away from food for good because she is an all-or-nothing person. She keeps vowing to be good again and diet even harder. The new diet leads to feeling more punished. Deprivation leads again to binging. Binging leads to more dieting—a vicious cycle that is non-productive and reinforces low self-esteem.

The second type of temper tantrum binge relates to emotions, especially anger or frustration, in the person's life situation. Binge eaters are usually nice people, non-assertive and accommodating. A binge is a way to "swallow" anger. Many people are able to stuff the anger so far down that they do not feel anything on a conscious level and just keep smiling. But the body is aware of the anger or resentment and learns to translate these unresolved and unacknowledged feelings into thoughts of food instead of thoughts of how to get rid of the problem. Thus the binger remains unconscious of the fact that a binge episode is a statement of inner feelings. It is as if the binge has a life of its own.

One woman tried to get her husband to be her "policeman." She wanted him to stop her from overeating. He refused. She continued her negative behavior, telling herself and the world, "See how helpless I am. Take care of me." Then she raged: "I always ask for too much from people who won't give it to me." She could excuse her overeating and blame it on her helplessness, or binge at her husband in retaliation for not rescuing her.

Whenever you have a binge, your first question must be: "What is going on in my life right now?" Some people binge at the same time every day. Ann binges and vomits after work (at a job she hates). The purge is her way of "puking" at someone or something rather than saying how she feels. Binges often reflect situations in which the binge eater feels victimized, put into a position she *thinks* she is unable to change. Beth would go to dinner with a girl friend and then come home to binge. She was frustrated as a result of her pretense of dieting when she was in public, refusing to eat as much as or what she wanted. She also felt angry because she was out with a woman and not a male date and had to come home alone. She told herself that she would never find a mate. She would be alone forever. Then she ate.

If you are a binge eater, you may tend to berate yourself for binging. Your may dwell on how much you ate and what you ate. You would be missing the point. The only way to stop this behavior is to understand that a binge is a direct reflection of what is going on in your world. The intensity of the binge reflects the amount of painful emotion you are feeling.

The type of food eaten often suggests what you need and are not getting or doing. Sweets "make nice" and are comforting. Some overeaters like to chomp down on nuts and crunchy foods rather than express anger verbally.

Some bulimics eat or drink foods that are easy to vomit or facilitate vomiting. They do not care a great deal about the taste. One woman who stopped vomiting had an overeating episode and decided to let it be. As she felt the discomfort of the fullness begin to dissipate, she realized that the vomiting symbolized her desire to keep herself from assimilating things, both on a food level and a living level. Giving up vomiting meant that she had made a commitment to experience life and deal with it directly.

FILLING THE VOID

Bingers often overeat to feed yesterday and tomorrow. Today never receives enough. They suffer less from gluttony than from starvation. The empty void that never gets filled can never be filled by food. Binge eaters thus turn to food when their needs are not being met.

Bulimics and anorectics often deprive themselves of the food they need to be healthy. The body may react with feelings of tiredness and unceasing hunger. Some people eat only junk foods, which lack vital nutrients. Many go the vegetarian route but because they lack information this diet causes depletion of their bodies' nutrients. The greatest number of binges reflect emotional deprivations, however, not food deprivations.

THREE BASIC NEEDS

Human beings have three basic emotional needs:

- Identity . . . *Who Am I?*
- Relationship . . . *Am I Lovable?*
- Power . . . *Am I in Charge of My Life?*

"*Who Am I?*" is a scary question for binge eaters. Instead of knowing themselves and asserting their own wishes, many people who abuse food have been knuckling under to others' wishes for most of their lives. I remember Alice, who went to school to get a Ph.D. in economics just to please her mother. Ever since childhood, she had loved music and wanted to be a professional musician, but her mother said that musicians were "hippies" and unreliable. So Alice gave up her dream. Every day that she had to go to her job, she overate. She was doing what someone else wanted, not what she wanted.

When I met Peggy, she weighed ninety-eight pounds and thought she was going crazy. She existed on a diet of juice and tea during the day at work and at night gorged on sweets, which she regurgitated. Peggy discovered that although she said she hated the comments and sarcasm from her fellow workers about her strange eating behavior during the day, she was secretly proud to be thought of as "Miss Perfect Dieter," thinner than everyone else. This was her identity. It seemed worth the pain of starvation to get attention as a "special" person. She came to see me when she had become ready to give up that unrealistic goal in favor of finding the real Peggy: warm, loving, humorous— a human being, not a clothes hanger.

The emotional need for *relationship* involves a variety of transactions from family interaction as a parent, sibling, or spouse to friendship and job-related activities. Relationship needs bring up the issues of getting love, warmth, friendship, affirmation of self, sex, affection, and unconditional acceptance by others. When a binge eater tells me that she has been out of control for a few days and can't figure out why she is eating, I ask her two simple questions. One: What is going on right now that is upsetting?

And Two: What needs do you have that are not being met?

Louise was working at a job that was interesting and paid well, but her boss constantly discounted her work. When Louise put a project together, instead of complimenting her on a job well done, he would point out any minor flaw that he saw. Every month or so, he would call Louise in and tell her that she did good work, but . . . and would erase the praise with criticism. After these meetings, she would eat for twenty-four hours.

Fanny had been divorced once and later remarried and was then widowed at an early age. She worked hard all day at a very demanding job, but at night, when there was nothing to occupy her time, she binged uncontrollably. Her binges had been going on for a long time. One night, before she put the first cookie into her mouth, Fanny had a sudden insight. She realized that as a forty-five-year-old woman, she was still young and still had sexual urges. She was terrified of men. After all, her first husband was unloving and critical, and her second husband had abandoned her by dying. The only way she could cope was to turn off the sexual drive before she felt it. Food served two purposes for her: it distracted her from her sexual feelings, and it comforted her and made her feel good. Fanny knew she really needed companionship, love, affection, and sex. Soon afterward, she decided to date again.

She began to accept invitations to be with old friends. Soon she was invited to small gatherings where she felt safe because she knew some of the people. With the help and support of her girl friends she started to go out on double dates with them and eventually found herself back in the social world.

Bulimics feel especially lonely and alienated from others because they fear that people will find out about their binge/purge behavior. Bulimic women usually have few intimate relationships. Even their parents or spouses are kept at a distance. I often get phone calls from young women who refuse to leave a phone number because they are afraid of who might pick up the phone when I return the call. This constant vigilance leads to stress and mistrust. Instead of feeling happy and excited on a date, some bulimic women tell me they can't wait to go home and eat and purge. The challenge of having to act "normal" in public is too taxing.

Power over one's life is an important issue for binge eaters. Their entire existence is a constant struggle between control and being controlled by others or by their appetite. The food issue is the battle. The body is the battleground. Feelings of powerlessness and self-discount keep the victim from speaking up. Because of such struggle, one woman finally ran away from home. She was unable to tell her family how she felt, so she had to act it out to give them the message. Fear of rejection, extreme sensitivity to what others think, and low self-esteem keep the binge eater from getting what she wants. She is never really full, but very, very empty.

Esther, an obese compulsive overeater, loved to paint as a hobby. Sometimes she would get lost in her creative project and her husband would come home from work before she could complete her housework. He often gave the house a white-glove test for dust and dirt. If things weren't perfect, he would scold her for not doing her work.

Besides, he hated the smell of her paints. One weekend, her husband took the children on a campout. Esther was able to stay home all alone. Her husband frowned on her frivolous activity, so she knew he wouldn't like it if she wasted her time painting. She just had to paint! So she painted her son's bedroom and the bathroom. I see Esther's behavior as giving away the power to be in charge of her life.

THE BINGE CYCLE

The addictive cycle to which the compulsive binger returns again and again can be broken down into a series of steps. Although a binge may seem to come out of the blue without rhyme or reason, there is a pattern that is the same each time. The cause of the binge may vary, but the episode is made up of these steps:

1. Trigger
2. Desire/decision
3. Action
4. Hangover
5. Letdown
6. Back where you began

The connection between the events of the day, relationships, personal attitudes, emotions, and the binge must be clearly seen by the binger before the recovery process can begin.

The trigger is usually an emotional feeling. This feeling results from a given situation in life. It can be a one-time experience or daily happening. Common feelings that lead to binges are anger, loneliness, rejection, resentment, helplessness, self-deprecation, depression, boredom, and even extreme happiness. These feelings may originate from the environment in which one lives or works. The time of day, time of year, and what is going on in the world all contribute to the decision to binge. Most important are the feelings that arise from interpersonal relationships or lack of meaningful relationships.

The trigger leads to the desire/decision to binge. Every binge eater I have talked with can remember making the decision. The desire to eat and the decision to follow through are the second phase of the binge process. Many binge eaters make the decision to binge hours before they actually do it. Some make an elaborate ritual out of shopping or preparing for the binge. A binge can also be put into action minutes after the decision is made. But first there must be a decision.

I have known people who eat in their sleep. One woman reported broiling steak and consuming it in her sleep. She was unaware of her behavior until the next day when she awoke to find the dirty dishes and pans. How could she have done it? Obviously, some part of her made the decision and carried it out. The unconscious mind never sleeps. It is interesting that sleep eaters do not eat diet food in their sleep.

Even though a binge eater may feel totally out of control during a binge, she is really making many decisions about what to eat. She may be in a frenzy, but she will hold out for what she wants. After she has devoured her first choice, she may then settle for whatever is at hand, but she is always evaluating and choosing what comes next.

Andrea, a bulimic who vomits, told me that she never binges on nuts because they irritate her throat when she purges. No matter how intensely she eats, even stealing food from her roommate, she always leaves the nuts.

Action follows the decision. It is at this point that each person performs her own individual ritual. The amounts of food eaten may vary dramatically from a doughnut to food containing as much as 50,000 calories. For bulimics, the action includes the total binge/purge cycle. The compulsive person performs these behaviors to experience a "high" or a "low." Many hypoglycemic bingers have reported eating quantities of sugar to maintain a "sugar high." In my practice, I observe that the majority of food addicts overeat in order to soothe, tranquilize, or deny negative feelings. Some eat and purge or overeat to the point of stupor. They crave oblivion and use food as a sleeping pill—a "downer."

The action event of the bulimic is twofold: the binge and the purge. The binge acts as a temporary analgesic— a frantic attempt to fill the void. The short-term effect of the binge is an immediate feeling of relaxation and relief. Andrea said that when she binges, the pain goes away. The binge serves to distract her from her feelings or problems. As she is swept along by her frenzied eating, she is also aware of her inability to stop. This is a negative aspect of the binge, which reinforces her belief in her lack of power and intensifies the fear of getting fat.

For bulimics, feelings of calm or tranquillity must quickly be followed by getting rid of the excess food in order to prevent weight gain. The very act of vomiting is extremely debilitating and leaves the person weak, sore, hoarse, often with broken blood vessels in the face. The purge often gives a sense of relief and a cleansing or purifying experience. A great many bulimics are very interested in good nutrition and health food, yet they binge on the junk they would normally deny themselves. This purging may be seen as a ritualistic act of self-punishment and expiation of guilt.

It may take hours or days to recover from a binge or a series of binges. For some, the aftereffects include a dramatic change in energy and personality. This is the hangover, and it may be both physical and emotional. Depending on the severity of the binge and resultant purge, the bulimic feels weak and may have a sore throat and hoarse voice. Many have scars on their hands from tooth marks and acid burns that result from forced vomiting. There may also be serious physical side effects such as electrolyte imbalance, kidney impairment, and rupture of the esophagus. The emotional hangover is continued guilt, self-hatred, hopelessness, helplessness, and depression. The binge eater may try to promise herself that she will stop tomorrow, try harder, or never eat junk food again.

After all is said and done, the overeater experiences a letdown feeling. Nothing has been accomplished; nothing has been learned. The situation that triggered the binge has not changed. The binger feels more unhappy, frantic, and depressed than before because another episode reinforces the belief that she is hopeless. She is now back where she began.

THE COMFORT ZONE

Sometimes the binge eater feels lonely, rejected, or victimized and does *not* overeat. After working with compulsive eaters for many years, I have observed that one of the major factors in a binge is the intensity of the feelings the person is experiencing.

There are ups and downs in everyone's life. Most people are able to weather the storms of illness, loss, disappointment, rejection, and loneliness. I call the range of happiness and misery you can live with, without becoming ill physically or emotionally, the "comfort zone."

Anxiety and unhappiness result when something extremely devastating occurs, such as the death of a loved one, rejection by a mate, or loss of a job. Some people find that the excessive positive energy or joy that derives from experiences like winning an award or being praised in public produces tremendous strain or emotional "pain." While a well adjusted person may have a comfort zone of plus 50 to minus 50, many binge eaters have a comfort zone of only plus 10 to minus 10 while others have an even narrower limit of plus 3 to minus 3 and therefore feel overwhelmed by life all of the time. When a binger endures pain of a positive or negative force beyond her comfort zone, she will attempt to stop the pain or eradicate the discomfort in the best way she can. People with eating problems turn to food to reduce the intensity of feelings.

Some situations that trigger binge feelings occur every day. Mark, a salesman, worked at a job that involved traveling around town. He was so efficient that instead of staying in the field until 4:00 p.m. he quit at 2:00 p.m., having accomplished a full day's work. His food diary revealed that he never binged until after 4:00 p.m. He realized that the afternoon binge was a combination of relief from an extraordinarily stressful job, which built up a great deal of negative energy during the day, and self-punishment for cheating his employers by leaving work early. Some of the eating was to relieve guilt at cheating and not getting caught.

Dancers often experience great stress at the thought of being fat or too stuffed to dance well. Eating a meal before performing seems to produce feelings of anxiety well beyond the comfort zone. Every day that Betty danced, she threw up her breakfast. Although she ate only vegetables, she explained that she felt too stuffed to feel her body and do well in dance class. Dr. L. M. Vincent in the book *Competing with the Sylph* describes the ritual followed by dance students who rush to the bathroom to throw up before the weigh-in at ballet classes. Fear of the scale and the disapproval of the teacher results in an often repeated activity that becomes a habit. The group binge or "pig-out" that follows is both a reward for getting through the ordeal and a way of deadening anxiety. This behavior parallels the antics of the dieter before getting weighed at the diet doctor's office. Like the ballet student, she often follows a weight loss with a congratulatory ice cream sundae.

Some individuals binge after being with a mother, a sibling, an authority figure, or someone they fear. Although they may have moved away from home long ago, many bingers revert to their childhood feelings and actions when they go home for a visit. The thirty-year-old lawyer is once again at the mercy of her overbearing father or critical mother who comments on what she is eating and how she looks, just as they did when she was thirteen years old.

Other causes for binge urges are specific and one-time events. Major holidays of the year or birthdays can trigger very strong feelings of loneliness, loss, or anger. Vi started craving nourishing food when the weather turned cool and the holiday season approached. Such food was a symbol of her mother and the sense of family that Vi had lost when she moved to another state.

Some people are able to realize that their increased binge eating or episodic binge/purge is in direct relation to increased stress caused by a recent development that pushes them beyond the comfort zone. Marian began to exhibit bulimic symptoms when her former husband contacted her to see about a possible reconciliation. Randi started to throw up when she realized that not just her job but her choice of profession was too stressful for her to remain in it. Her fear of being without a job or adequate income pushed her over the brink into throwing up for the first time in her life. Before this episode occurred, she had been a compulsive eater and dieter.

"Over and overs" are situations that you live with almost every day that can cause anxiety. After a while a bulimic may be so used to this unhappy state that she does not understand that her daily binge/purge is not just something she does but is triggered daily by the renewal of pain, like reopening a wound and putting salt into it.

Sandy is a dancer who started to vomit when she moved away from home to the big city to dance. The competition frightened her and, combined with her need to be perfect, triggered bulimic behavior. Every day that she took classes or competed for dance jobs her belief in her lack of perfection was reinforced. She lives with constant anxiety. She binges daily.

YOU CAN LEARN FROM YOUR BINGES

When a binger is willing to ask herself what feelings she might be avoiding or what situations or relationships are generating anxiety, she is taking a giant step toward recovery.

As most bulimics do, when we meet, Terry wanted to berate herself for her bulimic episode. Instead, I insisted that she be grateful for the awareness that brought her to the realization that she could learn something from the experience so she would never have to feel that way again. What feeling or event triggered her binge? Terry was angry with a man who did not give her what she wanted and needed: warmth and sex. Her latest boy friend gave her double messages; he encouraged warmth and closeness but pushed her away sexually. Terry's father had had custody of her when she was small. He acted loving some of the time, but he also picked on her and beat her with a large leather belt with a metal buckle. There was an intense push-pull in her relationship with him. She both loved and hated her father. After a disappointing date, she binged as an expression of rage at this other man who gave and then withheld love. She recalled that she had the same problem in most of her love relationships. Each lover had shown her a certain amount of love and acceptance but had also punished or discounted her much of the time. Her inability to express rage toward her father for his abuse had carried over into those relationships, and she again withheld expressions of anger toward those who were depriving her of happiness. She did not allow herself to meet men who would be unconditionally loving, only those who would cause pain—men like her father. Terry found out that stuffing herself with food was a way of stuffing down anger. The food symbolized comfort for her and also acted as a replacement for sexual pleasure.

Management of binge eating entails an examination of the binge behavior from different points of view. The key to change lies is the ability of the sufferer to become conscious of her decisions about her behavior and to link the behavior to its antecedents, her feelings about life's situations, and her relationships with others.

The binge eater needs not only to recognize the feelings that trigger a binge but to learn to handle them without denial or avoidance. She needs to learn new options for problem solving and assertive skills.

CAN A BINGE BE GOOD?

All binge eaters tell themselves that binges are "bad." Did it ever occur to you that a binge could be good? A binge may be a blessing in disguise. A toothache is a signal that something is wrong in your mouth. A binge is a signal that something is wrong in your life. If you have a toothache, you will most likely go to your dentist as quickly as possible to have it taken care of. And if you suffer from recurring headaches or stomach pains, sooner or later you will begin to worry and check it out with a doctor. Pain is your body's way of telling you that trouble or dis-ease exists. Most of us need that warning and then take

71

necessary action to get rid of the underlying cause of the pain. Bingers tend to have difficulty recognizing signals, instead using the binge behavior to cover up and not feel the pain or notice the signal.

A binge is like a red flag waving a signal. The behavior is telling you that you are feeling disease or emotional pain. It is not the food consumption that is the problem. You are neither a good nor a bad person for binging. You are simply a person in pain who is ignoring the pain. The pain may increase. It certainly will not go away unless you get to the source of it.

Binge eaters look at their problem from the wrong perspective. They focus *only on food*, not on *feelings* and *stress-producing* situations. Many of my clients try all the diet programs that are available. Some go to nutritionists or weight-loss clubs. Jean came to see me because she was on a medically supervised fasting program, but she kept breaking the fast and binging. She knew very well why she ate. She was upset because she was losing weight too quickly. It scared her that she might reach her goal before she was "ready."

Jean was not "ready" to be slim because she was not sure what to do about her career. She believed that when she reached her goal she would be obligated to know what her life's goals were and how to achieve them. She thought she should be unafraid and assertive, strong and beautiful, but she was far from that and she was losing weight so rapidly that she was sure she would never be emotionally ready when her body was ready for her new life.

Sharon lost sixty pounds on a fasting program and began an immediate sixty-pound weight gain after her first date as a thin woman. At the age of thirty-five, she has never married and is still ambivalent about men and the nature of intimate relationships. Her fat is her protection. She uses it as an excuse for not dating or getting seriously involved. Vickie, on the other hand, had no trouble finding dates although she weighed over two hundred pounds. She was afraid of being thin for a different reason. Her career was in show business. If she lost weight she would have to show everyone that she could be a star. As long as she was fat, she could use her weight as her rationalization for not looking for or getting the "right" job. She was afraid of what others would think if she were thin and still a failure. Brenda had a different story. She shared with me that she lost fifty pounds on a crash diet and regained it quickly. Then she discovered that she thought she needed to be fat in order to "throw her weight around" in the world.

No amount of dieting or fasting will make you stop binging. Binges are the result of denying your feelings and not confronting and resolving the problems in your life. As you raise your self-esteem, you can learn to ask for what you need, take care of yourself, and assert yourself. As a result of positive action on your part, your binges will become fewer and smaller in quantity of food consumed. But they will not go away by themselves. You need to know that a desire to binge is a reminder of a problem you are not heeding. In order for you to be free of compulsive overeating, you will have to modify or change your behavior around food in a conscious way.

I: Food Addiction: A Problem for Millions

FEAR OF FOOD

One possible side effect of a lifetime of dieting is the fear
of food. Even after you deal with big issues in your life,
you may still be hampered by myths and magical beliefs
about what you can and cannot eat. Many compulsive
overeaters believe that they are allergic to sugar and will
break out with compulsive cravings if they eat refined
carbohydrates—and they do. Is it a physical truth or is it
a self-fulfilling prophecy? Cynthia warned me that she gets
"set off" by cheese. I don't need to figure out how each
person forms these idiosyncratic eating fears, for they are
usually based on irrational beliefs. The general process
seems to work like this: the more you tell yourself that you
can't have a certain food, the more precious it becomes.
Then you find yourself obsessed with thoughts of it,
plotting to get it, cheat for it, steal it, taste it. Overeating
the food after a long period of going without it reinforces
your feelings of deprivation. Your gluttonous behavior is
proof that "I can't eat just one."

Bulimics have an enormous fear of food. There seems
to be one neutral food that many use as a free food or
safe stuffer. That food is popcorn. Because they are often
attempting to go for long periods of time without eating
but get too hungry and give in, some binge/purgers will eat
large quantities of popcorn and not throw it up. Popcorn
is low in calories when air-popped and is thus considered
a diet food by some bulimics. In addition to avoiding
high-calorie foods, bulimics are wary of the amounts of
food that they eat at one time. Anorectics and bulimics
often report that they feel panicked by the full feeling they
have after eating. They become emotionally upset by the

74

physical distress. This leads to an urge to get rid of the food immediately in order to get rid of the feeling of having food in their stomachs. A bulimic may purge after eating what others consider a normal dinner. Some bulimics I have treated allow themselves to eat only one portion of one food. They consider eating a serving of chicken and vegetables with salad and a beverage too much. The definition of a binge is purely individual. It is not a matter of amount but a matter of belief. The woman who eats a bowl of vegetables and rice, and throws up, feels as uncomfortable and emotionally stressed as the person who consumes twenty dollars' worth of food at one sitting.

In a therapy group, two bulimic women were talking about their food fears. One exclaimed that she loved to eat healthy foods like vegetables and chicken but hated herself when she pigged-out on ice cream. Another group member explained that she ate ice cream, frozen yogurt, and junk food all day long but was terrified to sit down at a meal of "real" food. A piece of chicken reminded her of what she was served at her mother's table. At that table people were urged to overeat, and the whole family was overweight. Therefore, she viewed "real" food as fattening. She was amazed at her friend's good feelings about healthy foods, so she decided to buy one chicken breast at the food-to-go counter of the market. She had the clerk weigh the piece to be sure it was small enough. It was a great risk for her to eat the chicken breast and not feel as if she had to follow with a binge because she had overeaten and might as well go all the way. She had turned down dates in order to avoid having to sit in a restaurant and order a complete meal, because of her fear of gaining weight and becoming undesirable. She was afraid of ordering small portions á la carte because she didn't want to appear strange and call attention to herself as a problem eater. Her dilemma was that if she did the "normal" thing and had a dinner, she would tell herself that she was binging and the "real" food would make her fat. This led to feelings of great anxiety. To please her date, she would have to overeat. If she pleased herself and ate almost nothing, she believed he wouldn't like her, and she would feel equally anxious about being rejected. Her solution was to avoid the entire situation by not dining with anyone.

After eating the chicken breast and discovering that it didn't produce a binge, she continued to add small portions of healthy food to her diet. She felt better physically as a result of eating more balanced meals with fewer refined carbohydrates. She is now able to eat "real" foods without fear, go out with others and eat part or an entire meal without binging, and laugh when she looks back to how she used to be. Ice cream is not a bad food nor is chicken. It all depends on what you tell yourself. You've probably heard the old saying "One man's meat is another man's poison."

Bulimics also have strong food preferences based on their purging styles. Some foods are difficult to throw up. Others are easier. For this reason, some bulimics binge on soft, creamy foods like ice cream or milk rather than nuts and coarse foods. One bulimic always started a binge with healthy foods such as meat or vegetables. She would then gorge on junk foods. Her rationale was that when she vomited, the first foods eaten would be retained and give her the basic nutrition she needed in order to avoid malnutrition and electrolyte imbalance.

Food fears are based on diet mythology. The diets of twenty years ago forbade certain foods that are good for you. Baked potato and bread or grains are shunned or feared by a multitude of binge eaters (when they are being "good"). Yet these foods, eaten in moderation, are healthy for your body. Nutritionists have problems getting their clients to overcome the feeling that eating bread is tantamount to breaking the diet.

BINGE FOODS

Foods that trigger binges are also individually chosen. Not all binge eaters turn to sweets for a binge, although the majority do. Many prefer salty foods such as pretzels and chips. Bingers who will eat anything that is handy when they are in the throes of compulsive eating are in the minority. Binges are usually made up of foods the binger tells herself are bad, or junk, or forbidden "forever." Very few binge eaters believe that fish or spinach or broccoli are fattening. Therefore, eating these foods does not produce guilt. Others are upset by the size of portions. One binge eater told me that she had been very bad because she ate two cookies. Cookies are unacceptable; therefore, any cookie eaten means the rules have been broken.

The choice of foods to binge on varies as dramatically as the number of calories consumed. Although a small percentage of bingers eat anything that they can lay their hands on, most have specific cravings. Sometimes these foods represent larger categories such as breads, cookies, fast foods, or fruits. Some binge eaters crave a more specific food such as chocolate kisses, french fries, chocolate cream pie, or even certain brands of food. These foods usually represent a link to the past, a quality of nostalgia. The food is a symbol of a pleasurable experience that is long gone.

Once the binge begins, the taste of the food becomes less important than the speed with which it is consumed. After the first few mouthfuls, the binge eater barely chews or stops to enjoy the flavor or texture. Rather, she has a need to fill up, more and more quickly, to fill the void, the emotional blackness.

The state of mind of the binge eater in the midst of a binge is like that of a person in a daze. All outside distraction is turned off. There is only the act of finding and eating food and more food. The compulsion to continue overrides any attempt to think about stopping. One woman likened her binge experience to riding an escalator: once you get on, you can't get off until it reaches the next floor. Even as you are aware that you have begun the trip (or binge), you cannot turn around and go back or get off in the middle. You may not be able to stop yourself in the midst of an overeating splurge, but as you work on understanding what sets you off emotionally, you will be able to stop yourself before it begins. The more you work on accepting a binge as a signal of emotional turmoil, the sooner you will find that your binges are smaller and less intense. The important thing is to evaluate every binge afterward and to learn from each one.

If you binge long enough and intensely and become overweight, you may, instead of looking into the truth of your behavior, spend years in passionate dieting and failure (regaining the weight). If you gorge and purge you will not have to diet but may become obsessed with the fear of getting fat, so you diet as a preventive measure. Again, the diet becomes the surface issue while the real issues are buried.

A diet is a detour. Look at the binge. Every binge makes a statement. In this book I will teach you to decode the message of your binges and explore the life problems most characteristic of all food addicts.

MEDICAL DANGERS OF EATING DISORDERS

Even though eating disorders such as anorexia nervosa and bulimia are symptomatic of unresolved psychological problems, they can cause serious medical complications. Among the physical consequences of long-term binge/purge or binge/fast episodes are gastric problems, kidney damage, abnormal metabolism, dehydration, muscle spasms, bleeding of the throat, and chemical imbalance leading to cardiac arrest. The majority of binge/purgers who come into my office have not mentioned to their doctors that they are concerned about food. Many complain of tiredness while affirming that they think they are OK when questioned about physical health and well-being.

The truth is that extended periods of starving, fasting, or purging by vomiting, laxatives, or diuretics can and often do lead to severe medical problems—even death. If you are, or have been, binging and fasting or binging and purging on a steady basis, the first step you need to take is to visit a doctor you can trust. Your family doctor may not be the right one for your to see if he is not familiar with the medical aspects of eating disorders. You may want to contact your local medical association or teaching hospital to get referrals for the best and most informed sources for your problem.

If you trust your doctor and feel good about talking to him, be sure to give him complete information. Describe your behavior: what you do, how often, and for how long you have been eating and purging, or binging and dieting. Be sure to tell your physician what drugs or medications you take and whether you have been using diet pills, diuretics, laxatives, alcohol, or street drugs. The hardest part of getting over your eating disorder may be gaining the courage to tell someone else about your behavior. Your body may be suffering from problems directly related to your binging, and you may not be aware that your internal organs have been damaged. Certain medical tests are mandatory to give your physician and you a clear picture of the state of your health and to help the doctor clear up any physical side effects.

Two routine tests you may be familiar with are the complete blood count or CBC and urinalysis. These tests will give your doctor information about your general health. In addition, it is imperative to have your blood electrolytes checked. When the electrolyte balance is disturbed, serious trouble ensues. The two most important electrolytes that anorectics and bulimics should be aware of are sodium and potassium. The blood test for electrolytes will also measure chloride and carbon dioxide in your body. Your doctor should order liver function studies to complete the picture of general body function relating to nutritional deficits.

People who have undergone crash diets, intense fasting or starving, or purging can die from a drop in serum potassium. Low levels of serum potassium can result in kidney failure and cardiac arrest.

Excess use of diuretics is dangerous and can lead to electrolyte impairment. Appropriate amounts of water are necessary to maintain healthy body function. Your doctor may think that an electrocardiogram (EKG) is indicated if you have been a long-term and intense purger or if your blood pressure or pulse are not in the normal range.

SIDE EFFECTS OF VOMITING

Some vomiters notice a swelling or pain in the parotid or salivary glands. Excessive purging often causes a "chipmunk" look because the cheeks swell. This is caused by the elevation of an enzyme called serum amylase, which is secreted by the salivary glands. The skin may become dry because of dehydration resulting from excessive fluid elimination.

Teeth can be dramatically affected, too. Many bulimics spend huge amounts of money at the dentist. Frequent vomiting causes extensive cavities and erosion of the enamel of the teeth. Inadequate diet, diet limited to citrus fruits, or binges containing abnormal amounts of carbohydrates can also be destructive.

WATER RETENTION

Water retention or edema is a common complaint of all binge eaters. Edema may be related to electrolyte imbalance because you may be suffering from malnutrition as a result of starvation or prolonged dieting. Frequent vomiting, laxative, or diuretic abuse will also contribute to edema or bloating.

Sodium and potassium are the two main minerals that regulate fluid balance in the body. Potassium is concentrated on the inside of the cell, and sodium is concentrated on the outside of the cell. To maintain fluid balance, you need a certain amount of each of these substances within and without the cell. If you deplete your potassium levels by vomiting or other means of purging, you can cause a shift of the fluids from the inside to the outside of the cell. As fluid accumulates on the outside of the cell, obvious swelling occurs. Compulsive overeaters who do not purge also suffer from swelling after binges. Foods high in sugar or salt are usually favorite binge foods, and sugar and salt both have a tendency to promote water retention.

In addition to swelling in the face and feet caused by water retention, many anorectics and bulimics are troubled with abdominal bloating. Anorectics who have restricted the intake of food for a long time can suffer from an impairment that delays the emptying of the contents of the stomach. An uncomfortable feeling of fullness and bloating may result. The stomach may actually stick out. This can be a terrifying experience for someone who is frightened of getting fat. It is also normal to feel somewhat full after you have eaten. It is also normal to experience a slight distention of the stomach after a meal. This symptom will disappear with time. Part of the problem is the emotional panic that results from the bulimic's fear rather than the actual physical discomfort. People who have gone through long periods of fasting as well as those who are vomiters or laxative abusers may have to seek the help of a doctor to understand and get through the difficult period of discomfort and bloat that often occurs while they are learning to eat appropriate foods and larger amounts of food.

ABDOMINAL PAIN

Abdominal pains and gas also plague many bingers. This symptom can be the result of overeating. The amount and types of food consumed may lead to an upset stomach. A great number of bulimics, like their anorectic counterparts, attempt to go without food for long periods of time. The abdominal pains actually may be hunger pangs which are being denied or ignored. Pain may be a result of bowel irritations or effect of chemical imbalances. As the recovering binge eater begins to eat more regularly and more healthful, she may also suffer from gas or pain as the digestive system reacts to the new regimen.

CONSTIPATION

One of the most common physical problems encountered by people with eating disorders is constipation. A popular misconception is that a daily bowel movement is normal and that less frequent elimination is constipation. This is not true. Human bodies vary, and many people who are normal have bowel movements less often than every day. Some laxative abusers and vomiters have a history of constipation and digestive problems including colitis. These individuals are overly sensitive to the discomfort of the full feelings that comes when they eat normal or large amounts of food. Because they do not digest and eliminate the food as promptly as they expect, they resort to laxative use. Laxative abusers and people who vomit to get rid of the "stuffed" feeling need to know the dangers they risk.

For anorectics and bulimics who diet strenuously or fast, one of the major reasons for constipation is that they are not taking in sufficient food or liquid to form a stool. If not enough goes into the body, how can anything come out? Another cause of constipation is a diet that is too low in fiber (the indigestible part of the food which the body must eliminate). The result is that the body can create only hard stools that do not move through the digestive tract easily.

A diet high in meat, processed foods, and refined carbohydrates or grains is easy to digest but may lead to constipation problems because these foods pass through your small intestine and leave only a small residue for the colon to excrete. The colon is a large, muscular organ and must squeeze itself down to a very small tube to push the meager amount of waste along. Progress will be slow and may be accompanied by abdominal pain. It is desirable for the body to produce a bulky stool that is full of fiber, which attracts fluid. The colon then needs only to contract slightly to move the stool along easily and swiftly.

Since binge eaters are usually on low-carbohydrate diets in between binges, they do not eat the whole grain products and other foods that would help to overcome this problem. Brown rice, fresh fruits, and fresh vegetables also provide fiber but are not always eaten often enough or in the right amounts.

Most doctors and nutritionists do not like to advise laxatives, even herbal ones. One of the side effects of long-term laxative use is that the bowel can lose its ability to move naturally. The bowel becomes flaccid, unable to function without artificial stimulation. Check with your doctor to see if a stool softener or an artificial bulk product would be a better solution than laxatives. Some drugs that are not laxatives can help speed up the digestive process. Again, your doctor will know if these are right for you.

There are three other solutions that a person suffering from constipation can try without medical help. Stomach exercises *in moderation* will help you help yourself. A *reasonable* exercise program can be beneficial if you are also changing your diet. The key words are *reasonable* and *consistent*. If you eat and keep down foods that are high in fiber every day, you should begin to feel changes in a short time. Drink plenty of water, too. If your body is dehydrated, the contents of your digestive tract will dry out as well. Finally, one of your best tools is time. If you persist, the bloating and discomfort will go away as your internal system revitalizes.

Some bulimics prefer to avoid the issue of constipation and abdominal discomfort by not eating. They think that if they don't eat, they will have no problems. These people need the reassurance of a doctor or health professional as they go through a relearning period.

MENSTRUAL PROBLEMS

The loss of menstrual periods and menstrual irregularities are another area of concern for female anorectics and bulimics. The cessation of the menses is related to the amount of weight and body fat that is eliminated through starvation or crash dieting. There is a direct relation between the proportion of body fat and hormone production in women.

Recent research has shown that a critical amount of fatty tissue is necessary in the female body before a girl can start to menstruate. The growth spurt experienced by adolescent girls, in which half of the weight gained in subcutaneous fat (which adds to the curves of the female form), appears to trigger various hormonal systems that must function before menstruation can begin. During puberty, girls add body fat so that they have twice as much in proportion to adolescent boys. Although the modern woman or girl may try to hide or eliminate this fat, it is essential for physiological maturation and fertility.

For bulimics who are normal weight, purging plus emotional stress may play a great part in causing the menstrual problems. The average woman experiences some irregularity in her cycle because of emotional upsets at some time in her life, and anorectics and bulimics are in a constant state of stress and anxiety.

NUTRITION AND EATING DISORDERS

It is hard to imagine that malnutrition might be a problem for a middle-class woman, yet anorectics and bulimics risk this possibility regularly. They may gorge; but when they purge, they deprive their bodies of necessary nutrients. The result is a strange and unnecessary contradiction: starving amidst plenty.

The first step on the road to recovery for a bulimic is to make sure the foods she keeps in her stomach contain the proper nutrients for healthy living. Some bulimics eat and throw up everything they have eaten because they feel too full. Others eat healthy foods in small quantities and purge only their binge foods. It is important to focus on effective nutrition. Three important food groups to include in your diet are whole grain products, fresh fruits, and fresh vegetables. In addition to carbohydrates and fats, the average young woman needs approximately 46 grams of protein a day.

Dieters tend to forget that foods often thought of as containing primarily carbohydrates also contain protein. The body can use grains, dried peas, and legumes eaten together with milk and cheese as efficiently as animal proteins. Because of the danger of chemical imbalance, you may need more information about the nutritional content of the foods you eat.

Potassium is vital in human nutrition. According to the U.S. Department of Agriculture, the following foods are highest in potassium (contain more than 500 mg. per 3 1/2 ounces): avocados, lima beans, beet greens, garden cress, parsnips, and peanuts. Potatoes and spinach are also high in potassium. Many of my clients have discovered that when they change their overall nutritional intake, their emotional well-being improved and they had more energy.

THE EFFECTS OF SUGAR ABUSE

The choices of food can lead some people who binge to think they are hypoglycemic. Hypoglycemia is a condition of having a low level of glucose in the blood. Sufferers of hypoglycemia feel shaky and dizzy, cold and clammy, get hungry, experience anxiety, and many experience mood changes and psychological problems as a result of the change in body chemistry. To know if you are a hypoglycemic, you will need to be properly diagnosed by a competent medical doctor. He will probably give you a glucose tolerance test.

Many bingers think they are hypoglycemic, but actually they aren't. They do, however, have similar symptoms as a result of what binge eating does to their bodies. When you binge on foods high in carbohydrates (sugar), your pancreas will secrete insulin. Then one of two things can happen. If you are a vomiter, you may vomit all of the sugar away after the binge. No substance will remain for the insulin to act on. This situation will cause the remaining sugar to be taken up by the cells in a higher amount than they otherwise would have been. You see, once there is sugar in the stomach, the body secrets insulin. Even though you purge the sugar, the insulin has already been produced. The result of this unbalanced situation is a feeling of lightheadedness, anxiety, feelings of being cold and clammy, and even feelings of hunger.

If you don't vomit but use laxatives to purge, you will still feel shaky and sick, but the condition will not be as severe. Later on, after the cells take up the sugar, your blood sugar will drop below where it was before and you will feel hypoglycemic symptoms.

One of the myths of dieters and food abusers is that eating sugar leads to more craving of sugar. Sugar is not an addictive substance. There is no physiological proof that eating sugar leads one compulsively to eat more and more sugar. What happens is that the intake of sugar leads to insulin production, which leads to the sugar being taken up by the body, which leads to a drop in the sugar level, which can lead to hunger. Many people seem to hunger for sugar, but that may be either a learned response or a self-fulfilling prophecy ("I'm a chocoholic") rather than a physical reaction of the body.

In answer to the question, is the craving for carbohydrates psychological or biological, new findings show that the craving can be related to your body chemistry. Researchers have discovered that there is a chemical in the brain called serotonin which affects your appetite and your mood. When you eat carbohydrate foods, insulin is released into the blood. The amount of the amino acid called tryptophan is increased. Tryptophan controls the level of serotonin in the brain. When you crave sweets it may be because your brain is signaling for more serotonin. After the level has increased, the craving will abate. If you starve yourself of foods containing carbohydrates, you will be setting yourself up for periodic binges as your serotonin is depleted. Be aware that the brain also signals when you have had enough. Most bingers eat long after the desire to eat has disappeared. They eat until they are literally sick. If you keep eating and binging on sweets in this manner, you need to look into the behavioral and psychological aspects of binging.

GOOD NUTRITION IS REQUIRED

Balanced meals including foods containing fats, protein, and carbohydrates are desirable. Carbohydrates are digested quickly, and fats take much longer. Whole or solid foods will stay in your stomach longer than liquids. The longer it takes for food to pass from the stomach into the intestine, the longer your body will feel full. Eating only a partial meal or snacks will not satisfy you for long. Yet this is just the situation that some bulimics experience: they fear the feelings of fullness and satisfaction and yet crave those feelings at the same time.

To begin eating properly and to learn how to make informed and not irrational choices, you may want to consult a licensed nutritionist. If you are a binge/purger making the change to appropriate eating patterns, know that as you begin to eat, you do not have to gain any weight. Your body has the ability to burn up calories as you perform the tasks of each day. Even while you sleep, your body is using up calories for the pumping of your heart, circulation of blood, and workings of all your organs—it does this twenty-four hours a day. Your doctor or nutritionist can help you decide how many calories are right for you to maintain the appropriate weight for your height.

Binge eaters, like everyone else, need to consider the physical as well as the emotional aspects of their compulsive behavior. It is vital to consult with a knowledgeable doctor, who will understand the total picture and treat the disorder in a competent and caring manner.

II

*The World of the
Food Abuser*

A LIFETIME OF STRUGGLE: DIETS DON'T WORK

One of the central issues in the life of every food abuser is control. Each person who binges feels out of control. She worries about her food intake and fights to control the quantity and types of food she ingests, but food is only a symbolic arena for the greater issue of control over her life. Binge eaters may appear to be successful in careers or relationships. But at heart, the binger is a victim because she has given her power to some other person or agency and feels she has no control over her life.

Since anorexia nervosa is usually associated with adolescence, it is important to understand that the teen years are a time of growing up and separating from the family. The anorectic may want to remain a child in order to avoid the stresses and obligations of taking care of herself and being responsible for her decisions as a young

adult. Another possible factor in anorexia is that uncon-
sciously the family may want the youngster to stay childlike
and not grow up. Through her anorexia, the child is going
along with an unspoken message received from the parent
or parents. She behaves in a way that will keep her body
that of a child and also guarantee her a great deal of
attention from family members, such as a child would
receive.

Anorectics and compulsive overeaters exert power over
others in a subtle and passive way. The person who stops
eating or the person who binges is daring others to control
her. She leads them on a merry chase, all the while
proclaiming her inability to control herself. She gets time
and attention from the people in her life who work hard
to bring her under control or act as unwilling policemen
who watch over her and monitor her activities and food
intake.

Children are completely dominated by their parents
when they are young. Parents provide food, clothing, and
shelter, make sure the young one is safe, and teach the
child the skills needed to grow up. Much parental behavior
involves control of the child's behavior—what to do and
how to do it. There are two periods of rebellion, during
childhood and during adolescence: the toddler stage or the
"terrible twos," and the teen years. During each of these
times, the individual begins to see himself in a new way,
as a unique being, not a part of mommy and daddy but
alone and able to think for himself. Both the toddler and
the teen say and act out these ideas: the toddler through
the use of the reply "no" to everything that represents
parents, and the teen through behaviors and dress that
seem to oppose what his parents stand for or might wish.

There are, however, very good boys and girls who do not rebel. They learn to stifle the "no" and gain attention and appreciation from their parents by being perfect children. A great many of the food addicts I see do not really know who they are because they never have tried their wings and given themselves permission to be different. Frieda promised her dying mother that she would always be good. That promise became a terrible burden, but Frieda always smiled and forgave everyone and everything. She never lost her temper. Although she worked for a boss who discounted her and took advantage of her and was married to a man who abused her, she did not think she deserved anything better in life. She had learned to submerge her negative thoughts and feelings in food. She came to me because she could not stay on her diet. (Most of my clients first came to me because they were having trouble dieting.)

THE TROUBLE WITH DIETS

The trouble with diets is that they are temporary. You change your eating habits for a relatively short period of time—you suffer, you hold back, you use enormous willpower. All this control seems worthwhile because it won't last forever. Sooner or later (often sooner), you can go back to all the foods you forswore. Your old ways with food are right for you. Diets are unpleasant interludes in a life of food indulgence.

The trouble with diets is that someone else is telling you what, how much, and when to eat. A diet is a piece of paper with power over your life. If you keep eating by the clock or by the directions on paper, what are you learning? You learn that you can't do it yourself. You believe you need a supervisor or a policeman. But what happens when the policeman goes away? What happens when the diet is over? Who is there to keep you on the straight and narrow?

Whether a binge eater is thin or obese, she or he has been plagued by unhappy years of trying every new diet or weight-control fad that has come along. Thin binge eaters are seeking a way to stop binging, but the diets only deprive them more. Obese binge eaters want to lose weight, but diets challenge their insecurity about their self-control. More and more professionals now recognize that diets don't work. Losing weight is not the primary problem: the main issue is the abuse of food as a substance. Fat is a by-product of food abuse. In order to lose weight, the person must first understand the meaning of the food obsession as a symptom in her or his life. A diet merely postpones finding out what food really means to you and how it fits into your life-style as a source of pleasure or pain. Diets reinforce your beliefs that you cannot handle certain foods and that you are an irresponsible eater, a foodaholic. Diets keep you a victim of food forever.

When did this fantasy of helplessness around food start? I would bet that you are a very capable person. You may be a parent who knows how to take care of your child. You may own your own business, balance your own checkbook, shop for and prepare meals for others. So why are you such a dunce around food?

Many eating problems arise from the old-fashioned beliefs your parents held regarding how much food a baby needed, what kinds, and how often. One wonderful thing about the breast is that you cannot see through it. Babies are born with the ability to cry when they are hungry and stop eating when they are full. When a baby nurses, the mother has no way of knowing how much the baby has consumed. When the baby has had enough, he stops. As the baby grows and has growth spurts, he cries to nurse more often. The additional stimulation to the mother causes increased production of milk. The supply increases to meet the demand.

One awful thing about the baby bottle is that you can see through it. If the mother sees that there is milk left she may try to push the baby to finish. Many parents introduce solid food too early in hopes of getting the baby to sleep longer or through the night. This is a selfish aim that meets the need of the parent, not the child.

The child grows and learns to eat with the family. Many people had parents who put food on the plate and ordered the child to eat it, whether he was hungry or not. The clean plate syndrome resulted from the oft-repeated admonition, "Eat everything on your plate: the children in Europe are starving." Another common message was, "If you don't finish, you won't get any dessert." In many families, the child was given no choice about what or how much to eat. As time went by, the child gave up awareness of hunger and satiety and learned to obey the parents' demands. The grown-up was in charge. A diet is a symbol representing that person who told you long ago what to do. You still believe that someone else knows better than you.

Here you are, unable to control your life around food, but if you are on your way home for dinner with your four-year-old and pass a candy store, you can easily say no to your child. You remind the child that it is nearly dinner time and not time for candy. It is not amazing that overeaters can limit their own children but not themselves. You learned to be a parent by imitating your own parents. You can pass the rules and discipline that you learned on to your own kids. But you do not know how to parent the needy, greedy child within you.

That is the trouble with diets. The diet keeps you as a little child. It is a very arduous task to learn to be responsible for yourself. But what will you get out of owning your own body and being free of your feelings of helplessness? You will gain a feeling of power that you have never experienced before. Many bingers are afraid to feel good about themselves—to feel more assured, that they really know what to do and how to do it. They are afraid of giving up victimhood.

Many years ago I had a friend who was a member of a weight club. She had lost a great many pounds in the club and believed that without the group she would be lost and would regain all her weight. Her husband was transferred to another state and had to move to a city where there was no branch of the weight organization. She was so upset because she believed that she couldn't get along without her crutch that she convinced her husband to give up his job and move back to her home state and her weight club security.

CHEATING

The most uncomfortable aspect of a diet is the sense of deprivation that it fosters. Two kinds of diets are available today: the old-fashioned "grit your teeth and eat cottage cheese and hard-boiled eggs" variety and the personalized diets that allow you to have some cookies, ice cream, potatoes, and other treats.

A funny thing happened to a woman I met recently. She was under the care of a local nutritionist who designed a wonderful diet that included wine, desserts, and even a "Big Mac." Yet this woman kept cheating! No matter what she was told she could eat, some foods were prohibited, and she felt unable to resist them. Unless you have total freedom of choice, you may constantly feel deprived. In my classes, I often joke and tell my students that if I told them that they could eat anything they wanted except rye bread and pears, most of them would have an overwhelming craving for rye bread and pears in the coming week and would, most likely, cheat.

A diet sets you up to cheat. Even if you are on a deluxe personal plan, what if your diet for Tuesday calls for gelatin as a dessert and you don't really want gelatin? The diet perpetuates your belief that you don't know how to handle your own food choices. The majority of people I work with do the shopping and cooking for their families, yet their families maintain that those people are incapable of dealing with food and have to be "helped." Many anorectics and bulimics do the cooking for their families and are experts in nutrition and calorie counting.

The artificial nature of the diet may keep you full but not satisfied. Many dieters fill themselves up with lettuce and cabbage. They eat many foods that are ultra-low in calories—and also in taste. Although they are full, they are constantly hungry because they are not eating what they want but what they think they should have. The technique of filling yourself with no-cal foods or diet drinks fosters your fear of getting hungry. It supports your belief that you need lots of food and that, if you don't get it, you'll eat high-calorie foods and get fat.

In reality, when you eat a head of lettuce, you are still overeating because your stomach holds only two cups of food. You will be amazed at how great a feeling of satisfaction can come from eating a small amount of food that you truly want. Sally was terrified of sweets and had dieted without candy for years. She went to a fair and ate a small piece of fudge. It was so good that she felt no need to eat any more and even skipped lunch.

DIETS KEEP YOU HELPLESS

A diet teaches you to eat what you don't want and pretend that it is what you do want. This behavior reinforces a dissociation between your mind and body. Have you ever noticed that people without eating problems usually eat exactly what they want, stop when they have had enough— and do it unselfconsciously? Mind and body work together at all times if there is no interference by imposing the compulsions of distorted learning and beliefs.

A diet can also encourage you to eat when you are not hungry. A diet always mandates small amounts of food, but if you think that you have to eat breakfast after twenty-five years of never eating breakfast in the morning, you are overeating again! If you force yourself to follow an eating plan that tells you to eat three meals a day and some snacks, you will probably follow it because you are not going to let yourself eat less than you are allowed. If you are motivated, you will want to follow all instructions to the letter. But these instructions do not teach you how to make good decisions for yourself after the diet is over.

It is OK to skip meals. It is OK to be hungrier at some meals than at others. These are natural states that vary from person to person and day to day. Diets don't help you to realize when you are truly hungry or satisfied. Most dieters will eat the full allotment "because it is there." Every binge eater has had the experience of eating beyond the moment of "enough." So there is a spark of awareness in each overeater. A diet squelches this spark rather than encouraging it to light up your consciousness.

Diets are artificial regimens that are difficult to fit into your daily routine on a lifelong basis. When you diet you will eat many foods you don't want and almost none that you do want. You will eat at times when you are not really hungry and will not notice if you are satisfied but will eat until the food is gone. You will learn to fill yourself with filling and low-calorie foods in order to fill a void, not to stop true hunger. Who would want to or be able to continue this pattern of eating for a lifetime?

Diets serve to perpetuate the enormous fear of food experienced by bulimics and anorectics. Because diet programs avoid junk food and sweets, the person who already doubts her ability to renounce these items forever will feel even more helpless in the face of the powerful urge to binge on these very foods. Bulimics have very strict but often unrealistic ideas about certain foods. Even if a bulimic eats one small portion of a forbidden food, she may have to purge to rid herself of it because she believes that this will mean immediate weight gain. She has already told herself which foods are safe and which are dangerous.

Through persistent dieting she lives these thoughts as a formal affirmation of her irrational beliefs.

One young woman ate about 350 calories of safe food: yogurt, an apple, half of a bran muffin (a whole muffin may be considered an infraction of her rule), and salad. She filled herself up at night with popcorn. Bread was unthinkable; a baked potato was too frightening to contemplate; meat was to be eaten very carefully because it is too caloric and too tempting. Many binge eaters would like to be able to exist without eating at all so they would not be constantly confronted with the need to make decisions about food. But this idea is an outgrowth of the belief that they do not know how to deal with food and never will learn to be free of the bondage of food.

LEARN TO BE FREE

What is freedom? Freedom is the power to choose to eat or not to eat something without feelings of guilt. Freedom does not mean eliminating some foods from your experience forever; it means eating all or any foods in moderate portions without guilt. Freedom is the ability to stop because you have had enough, to leave food, and no longer to feel deprived around food.

Madeleine, a fearful bulimic, was invited to eat at a friend's home. Her friend had mentioned that she had baked a cake. Madeleine was torn between her desire for cake (a forbidden food) and her belief that she could not risk eating cake because one piece would lead to a binge. We talked at length about how she could change her attitude toward cake. I pointed out that she ate a bran muffin every day without feeling guilty or tempted to overeat. Madeleine had decided that bran muffins were a diet food, yet they contain many ingredients that are also found in cake. After thinking it through, Madeleine remembered that she had recently allowed herself to keep a small bag of chocolate kisses in the house. When she craved sweets, she had one kiss. She was able to eat one chocolate kiss and stop, but she could not imagine herself eating one piece of cake and stopping! Madeleine was free of fear and guilt about chocolate kisses. She can extend her freedom to cake when she is ready to tell herself that cake is OK.

Most binge eaters are free of guilt about and fear of spinach, green beans, cucumber, fish, and many other foods. Freedom comes from feeling relaxed and message-free about that food. Guilt will arise from messages about the food or of your being "bad." Only you can decide what is bad.

THE TROUBLE WITH FASTS

Fasts are a popular method of weight control. The trouble with fasting programs is that they, too, are temporary and artificial. People on fasts have one of two outlooks: either they are punishing themselves or they are delighted to be free of food. Those who think of the fast as an ordeal may have a hard time staying away from food and usually add to their unhappiness by cheating and feeling guilty about eating. They often quit the program before they reach their weight goal, feeling like failures, and usually gain weight back quickly because of the rebound from total deprivation from food.

The people who enjoy being relieved of the responsibility of making decisions about food feel euphoric and float along as if their feet were off the ground (nothing seems to trouble them) until they reach maintenance. They have a different problem at the end of the fasting process. When they return to the world of food, they must be re-educated to a new way of eating. But they were not able to practice new ways around food while they were fasting, so many of these successful fasters report enormous cravings and urges to binge. I have encountered some people who have fasted away as many as one hundred pounds and have turned to bulimic behavior, binging and purging in a desperate attempt to keep the weight off. After working so hard to shed the pounds, it can be a living nightmare to fight the cravings and overwhelming desire to eat nonstop.

DOCTORS AND DIETS

Another problem with diets is doctors. Many doctors have limited knowledge about nutrition or psychology. They may encourage or embarrass a patient into dieting but cannot reinforce the plan or understand the dynamics of their patients' problems with cheating. Many doctors jump on the bandwagon of the latest craze such as liquid protein or fasts with powdered protein. They rarely look into your psychological profile to see the possible stumbling blocks that might keep you from succeeding. Your physician will give you the proper blood tests and physical monitoring, but will he give you the emotional response you need? During the diet you may feel motivated because you are losing weight, but how will you handle a maintenance program? I have had a great number of referrals from doctors whose patients have lost fifty pounds on a supervised crash diet only to gain it back immediately.

You should approach a diet under a doctor's care cautiously. Check into the doctor's expertise, the number of times you actually will see him, and the success rate of his maintainers. Many clinics arrange for you to see the doctor once a month and a counselor weekly. Are the counselors professionally trained and experienced in working with the emotional problems relating to weight management? A fifteen-minute consultation with your weight counselor once a week is insufficient when you are trying to deal with the underlying stresses that trigger overeating or fears of giving up food or of becoming thin. Some effective clinics or programs provide a rap group for patients to attend during the diet program. Diet doctors will help you to remove the fat, but fat is not the primary problem; it is only part of a more extensive problem.

Here is a letter many of you would like to write to the doctors who have insulted you, browbeaten you, or intimidated you into losing weight. Some doctors reinforce the idea that the overweight person is stupid or a glutton. Many diet doctors see you infrequently and relegate your well-being to an assistant who weighs you each week and may distribute medication.

Dear Doctor:
I am a unique and special person, yet when you look at me you see me as a mound of flesh, a machine

that needs a tune-up or a valve job or new parts. You impersonally collect data about me through blood tests and tell me to lose weight. You give me diet, then you yell at me as if I am an incompetent child. You treat me as if I have no feelings about being fat. I want to please you while at the same time I want to spite you!

You give me orders to eat 600 calories. That is very scary. I am afraid I won't be able to keep to that diet, and then you will be angry with me. I cheat and hope you won't find out. I want you to make me thin, give me magic, be my friend. All you give me is lectures and impossible menus.

Doctor, please take your eyes off my chart and see me as a real person. I am not just a body. I have feelings, too. Help me set realistic goals. If I have to lose a hundred pounds, realize that it is like asking me to climb Mt. Everest. Help me to lose twenty pounds at a time. Please get to know me. Understand that losing weight requires taking a look at my life and my feelings. You don't seem to want to know about that or to help me deal with it.

See me as a person who will make mistakes. Allow for it. Praise my successes, no matter how small! Don't insult me, frighten me, or belittle me. Be compassionate. I am an individual. Help me to value myself. Help me to learn to be powerful over my body so your job will be easier. *Dear Doctor, Don't make me thin. Teach me to make myself thin!*

Sincerely,
Ms. X

THE SET POINT THEORY

Some of the most recent medical theories about how strict dieting can affect your body's tolerance for calories may be a strong argument against dieting. One theory explains that the body has what is called a "set point," which is like a thermostat. The set point is the weight at which your body will stay when you are not purposely either dieting or overeating. Your body will defend this set point weight even when you try to diet. Although you may be eating smaller amounts of food, the body will burn it up more slowly in order to keep you from losing the weight you are set at. This may explain why, even on the most stringent diets, after a few weeks the dieter begins to lose smaller amounts of weight. A number of those who have tried the liquid or protein fasts had weeks when they ate no food and lost no weight. One way that seems to lower your set point if it is too high for your taste is aerobic exercise, which will alter the metabolic rate and help you to burn up the food you eat more efficiently.

Although you may succeed in fighting against your set point and losing a large amount of weight, at the end of your diet your body will attempt to get the pounds back to the set point. This may account for the irresistible urge to binge that some dieters report after a crash diet. I find it interesting that many compulsive overeaters who have lost large amounts seem to regain it all and return to their original "home" weight.

I often have wondered why a person who used to weigh 228 pounds and lost 75 didn't stop at a weight gain of 50 pounds but went all the way back to 228.

The idea of the set point complements the theory that after years of dieting and regaining weight, you may have altered your metabolism so that your body cannot lose weight except on very small amounts of food. If it is not the food you eat but the activity and exercise you do that will affect your set point, constant dieting and deprivation may be pointless in the long run.

IS FOOD YOUR ONLY PLEASURE?

If you must diet, be sure to pamper yourself with non-food activities as much as possible to make up for the sudden lack of food pleasure that you will be experiencing. Give yourself many presents and nice times. Get into this new habit and continue it even after you have finished your program.

I once had a consultation with a woman who weighed two hundred pounds and was a binge eater. She wanted to lose weight. After taking her history, I discovered that her husband was in his own business and worked seven days a week. She spent an average of ten minutes a day with him. In addition to running the house and raising three children, she also handled part of his business, doing phoning and bookkeeping. They had not had a vacation in fifteen years. And because her husband had food allergies they rarely went out to a restaurant. She spent every day cooking, cleaning, and working . . . and eating. I told her that I thought it was ridiculous for her to try to lose weight at the time because food was her one and only pleasure, and I wouldn't think of taking it away from her. I assured her that when she developed a new set of pleasure-producing behaviors and activities that did not hinge on food, she would be ready to work on her weight.

Finally, diets don't help you to understand or overcome binge-eating behavior. They put you in a form of behavioral prison with special menus or food lists that eliminate binges because you are not allowed free choice. Every once in a while you may try to break out by "cheating." This break in your diet will be followed by feelings of remorse and unhappiness, and you will not learn a thing about yourself and what makes you eat.

Diets don't resolve compulsive eating behaviors: you are the only one who can do that. When you stop dieting, you will be able to learn how to make responsible choices for yourself. You already know all that you need to know about yourself, but you may have to do some work to find it again. The first step to undo the diet mentality is to make friends with your body, its sensations, urges, and feelings. You can learn to be in charge of what you do to and for yourself. You can use tools in this book to understand how binge eating plays an important role in your life and how to eliminate the binges and stop dieting. You will then become a person who knows her own limits and trusts them. It will take practice, but when you are free of binges, you can stay free.

CORE ISSUES OF
FOOD ADDICTS

-esteem, perfectionism, and conflict about sex
sexuality are troublesome for all binge eaters.
the individual is anorectic, bulimic, or a compul-
eater, she seems to be part of the same self-
and self-critical sisterhood.

very class I teach, I send around a sheet of paper
called the "Excuse Sheet," on which each student is to
write her excuses for not doing the work she contracted
with herself for: calorie counting, exercising, special writing
assignments, or self-affirmations. The most common excuse
is, "I was too busy." That is the excuse of the people-pleaser, the greatest single personality flaw of every food
abuser.

II: The World of the Food Abuser

PEOPLE-PLEASING

When you tell yourself that you will do what needs to be done for yourself later, after you have catered to the needs of everyone else, you are reinforcing the idea that you are less valuable than others. People-pleasing is the act of a person with low self-worth. She thinks she must buy approval through thoughtful acts and self-sacrifice. She soon earns a reputation as a dependable, wonderful person. The only trouble is that the people-pleaser is telling herself that her behavior is fraudulent and that, at heart, she is unlovable. She says to herself, "If they only knew the truth."

Many an anorectic or bulimic has developed overwhelming guilt when not taking care of someone else. Often, as a young child, she fantasizes that she must protect her mother or father and keep them happy at all costs. She pushes herself to become an overachiever and all-around good girl to avoid any situations that might rock the boat of supposed harmony in the family.

Obese overeaters are also people-pleasers. Many go out of their way to be helpful. They work overtime without asking for pay, and they sacrifice time and effort with a smile. But inside they are fuming with anger, feeling unworthy and unloved.

Kristi smiles a great deal and is solid, dependable, and motherly. She is tired of being so nice all the time. I asked Kristi to write a biography of herself as a "little mother." Here is some of what she discovered.

Take care of. That's the first step. Actually, the step is learning that you get certain rewards for "taking care of." Praise, "What a grown-up girl." "What a good, responsible girl, taking care of your brother."

Love and companionship, more rewards. Your brother loves you because you take care of him and comfort him when he is scared. You bind him to you. The cement of it is his dependence. Would you be that important to someone if they didn't depend on you for their needs? Would you be able to attract, to hold someone just by yourself without offering up your motherhood like a string of beads?

You learned to be the good girl, that's the way you do it with everyone. A good friend to all. Don't get mad; just be a good guy. If you get mad, you will deny someone your nurturing and you might lose them.

Be a good-guy lover. With a man, just supply. Forget what it is that you need. They just want someone to smile, to take care of them, to listen, listen, listen, to supply. Oh, what the hell, they're going to take off anyway.

The unanswered question for people-pleasers is *Who am I?* The food abuser tells herself that she knows who she is—she is an unacceptable, clumsy, no-talent, stupid, ugly person. She believes that she must continue to act out the role of a wonderful, creative, confident, achieving person to protect her inner flaws from discovery.

Leona, an attractive and sincere young woman who has been both a compulsive overeater and a bulimic, felt anxious because a man was paying attention to her and seemed interested in dating her. I asked what she was telling herself about the situation that led to her nervousness. She replied "What does he see in me?" I asked Leona if she had any friends who liked her and sought her company and what they liked about her. She could accept that her friends saw her as honest, reliable, and a good athlete, as well as a good listener. But Leona couldn't let herself think that these traits were really part of her. Until she believes in herself, she will find herself turning away the very thing she most desires: companionship and a relationship with a man.

Beneath every smiling, compliant, pleasing binge eater lies a dormant rebel. Anorexia—starving, or starving and binging—is an acting out of frustration and anger in the young person. Most parents who have wonderful people-pleasing children are lulled into complacency because they fail to recognize that the adolescent years are normally a time of quest for identity by the teenager.

Many teenagers act out the break from the bosom of the family through antisocial behaviors such as drinking, smoking, and taking drugs as well as breaking rules about sexual conduct. Some who are very bright rebel by doing poorly in school. Other turn away from their parents' religious or political view in their drive to find out the truth for themselves. In many families, understanding and love can help the child to make the transition from childhood to adulthood and be ready to assume a role as a healthy and well-adjusted person.

Food addicts, however, have either repressed their search for identity or were caught up in the idea that they had to be what others wanted them to be. I have known many people who have discovered, to their chagrin, that they married or chose a profession only to gain approval from their family and realized years later that it wasn't what they really had wanted for themselves.

Secretly, the binge eater long ago decided that in comparison to others she is not good enough, smart enough, pretty enough, or rich enough to compete with her peers. These decisions are often made in early childhood, and the parents are never aware of them. These distorted thoughts become part of the credo by which the food abuser lives. Every day becomes a struggle to win love and acceptance. She must prove herself over and over. But she continues to believe she is not acceptable.

Soon she focuses on the one objective that will symbolize self-worth—a "perfect" body. All her attention and most of her energy is turned toward dieting or exercising to reach the goal. Her irrational belief is that if she is perfect to look at, she will be OK. The unhappy girl tells herself that all her shyness and insecurity will vanish if she looks great. Soon the quest becomes an obsession.

One of the hardest positive things for a binger to do is to accept compliments or gifts. Many compulsive eaters can give freely to others but can't let others give to them. One way to change this habit is to "bite your tongue" when someone says something nice. Refrain from explaining why the compliment is unnecessary. Just let the kind words wash over you. At first, it will feel uncomfortable and awkward. You may be aware of inwardly rejecting such nice things. As time goes on, you will be able to receive more graciously and even feel good when another recognizes something positive about you.

THE STANDARD OF LIVING

Most individuals suffering from eating disorders have a lowered "standard of living." Everyone is familiar with the phrase *standard of living* as it pertains to the material things in life.

The "standard of living" pertains to one's emotional level as well as to material lifestyle. When you get out of bed in the morning you take many things about yourself for granted. You never question your name, address, and sex. Do you get up and dread the day because you have a "standard of living" that expects hardship and struggle, or do you rise and smile because you expect to live this day enjoying the best life has to offer?

Have you ever noticed that you know people who always have friends and things to do and others who are lonely and believe that it is hard to make friends? Some think of themselves as lucky; others call themselves unlucky.

Isabelle considered herself attractive to men. Her "standard of living" included dates anytime she felt like going out. Isabelle expected to go out, and she did. Candi was very attractive but couldn't seem to meet and date men. She believed that men were untrustworthy and would hurt her. She also believed that because she had once been a fat teenager, she was still unappealing even though she had lost weight and maintained her weight loss for years.

The "standard of living" about happiness varies greatly. Many bingers believe that because they have a terrible problem, they don't deserve to have the happiness and peace of mind that they think others have. Therefore, many of them settle for jobs and love relationships that are unfulfilling. They affirm that they are not as talented as their fellow workers and not as exciting or beautiful as other women, so they should be content with their lot.

These people fail to realize that they invite less than the best because they cannot give themselves permission to visualize a better life. I am reminded of a story told by a minister about a woman who came to him for counseling. She explained that she knew she had a "poverty consciousness" and was tired of being poor. She wanted to invite prosperity into her life but didn't know how. After they talked a while, the minister reached into his pocket and pulled out a ten-dollar bill, which he offered her. She recoiled and said, "Oh, I can't accept that!" That is the point: even if what you want is handed to you, if you have a lowered "standard of living," you either won't recognize it or you won't accept it.

To raise self-esteem, the binge eater must first be aware that she has a "poverty consciousness" about herself. Then she has to work to accept an alternate and happier "standard of living." She needs to realize that she pushes away the "ten-dollar bills" of love, approval, and opportunity in her life because she doesn't think she merits them. Then she must practice expecting more out of life and accepting more when it is offered.

As the problem eater begins to value herself, she will often be amazed that there are many situations and relationships she no longer feels comfortable with. She will begin to speak up and feel better about not settling for less than her new "standard of living" that attracts health and happiness.

PERFECTIONISM AND SELF-DEFEAT

Perfectionism is one of the most widespread and self-destructive aspects of the personality of the food abuser. In this era when an increasing number of women are in competition with men, women often view success in personal terms of sex and beauty. To compete, they must be perfect—and perfection is being *thin*.

The trouble with the drive for perfection is that you have only two choices: perfection or failure. Most perfectionists do not allow for other categories: high achievement and excellence. There are many achieving and outstanding people in the world who are not perfectionists. They allow themselves to make mistakes and sometimes to fall short of a goal without thinking that they are bad or unworthy. A perfectionist confuses the value of the product with the value of self. If the product is less than perfect, the person is less than perfect. The perfectionist applies a reverse double standard, accepting less in others but not in herself.

Because she is telling herself that there is only perfection or failure, she is anxiously judging herself.

A teenager bulimic named Sheryl was torturing herself because she thought she was too fat to wear a bikini. Yet she was eager to appeal to a boy whose looks were far from perfect. He was on a school varsity team and was extremely shy. His low-key personality and his so-so looks were of no importance to Sheryl, who liked him for other reasons. The thought that a boy could like her for reasons other than her looks was beyond her comprehension.

Perfectionists, like people-pleasers, are always looking to others for judgment and approval. The perfectionist always thinks she can do better and will not tolerate less than her best. These beliefs are taught by an authority figure, most likely a mother or father. "You should do better" or "Only a B+?" are criticisms that form a perfectionist.

I recently asked a perfectionist what projects she allowed herself to do less than a perfect job on. She replied, "Those that others won't see." The first person to judge your work was usually a parent. If that person was critical and rarely praising, you will learn to feel inadequate about yourself and your abilities.

Many parents have doubts about themselves as people or as good parents and are afraid that the world will find out their secret inadequacies. To keep everyone believing that they are great, they must have wonderful, obedient children. Therefore, the parent stresses high standards and unrealistic expectations, often overlooking the human flaws that exist in every person. The child is required to live up to the parents' expectations of what is "good" in dress, school, behavior, manners, and outlook.

Many children of critical parents try to turn themselves into clones. Dora was 5 feet 7 inches tall, and her mother was 4 feet 10 inches tall. Dora looked like a beautiful, slim woman, but she always felt too fat. She had spent most of her life comparing herself with her petite mother, who invariably found fault with her. Dora was not petite but thought she should be. If she were tiny and pretty, maybe her mother would accept her and stop telling her what was wrong with her looks. There was no way Dora could be her mother's twin, but she would not accept that she was entitled to look different and still be considered pretty.

Shoulds and shouldn'ts plague the perfectionist. There is no room for error. Instead of being able to review her eating behavior and focus on understanding how her eating binges reflect her life problems, the perfectionist will tell herself, "I should have known better" or "How could I have let myself binge?" Berating herself for her imperfect eating habits, she loses sight of the concept that a binge is a cry for help.

Most perfectionists will recoil at the idea that they, like everyone else, are always doing the best they can, *under the circumstances*. Knowing better and doing better are two different things. We all can find times when we could have done better, but we have to accept the limitations that prevented better results. Perhaps you had a headache or got too little sleep the night before. You may have had a fight with your spouse or had car trouble.

Perfectionists often have trouble with setting priorities. I have seen many people who are as upset about spoiling a dinner casserole as by losing a job. If the individual must be perfect all-around, everything is important. This attitude leads to constant anxiety, because she must juggle many areas of her life at once, without dropping the ball. She may find it difficult to let up on a minor problem and concentrate on a more important goal. All-or-nothing styles of thinking must be eliminated and a more loving and reasonable approach substituted. It may be necessary for the perfectionist to work with a therapist to retrain her behavior and her thinking.

Guilt, anxiety, and frustration result from self-punishing thoughts and reinforce the perfectionist's belief that mistakes are unacceptable. Countless emotional eaters have binged after stepping on the scale and not seeing a weight loss after a week of intense dieting. The expectation that if they are perfect they *have* to lose weight can lead to increased feelings of failure and hopelessness.

Diets perpetuate these negative thoughts. If a binge eater takes a bite that is not on her diet, she tells herself that she broke the diet and might as well continue to eat. Again, the polarity of all-or-nothing, good-or-bad seems to prove to the perfectionist that she is a loser.

TIME MUST BE USED CORRECTLY

Another facet of perfectionism has to do with attitudes about time and productivity. Doing nothing equals wasting time for the majority of binge eaters. They do not permit themselves to waste time. Time must be used and a measurable result produced. I recall a bulimic who had to schedule every hour of her day to refrain from binging and purging. One day she finished an appointment early and had two hours on her hands. She went on a two-hour binge. She told herself that she had to be industrious or she was bad.

What is a waste of time? The answer varies from person to person. For some, watching TV or reading is a waste of time. For others, resting or meditating is a waste of time. Most of my clients can lie down only when they are truly ill.

Ellie came to see me and brought her food diary. She had had a very slow week as a sales rep and was feeling insecure about her abilities and about generating the necessary income to pay her bills. I noticed that she had binged on Sunday, and I asked her what had happened. She told me that it was her day off, and, contrary to her usual habit, she stayed home and moped and ate although she usually enjoyed her days off and saw friends. After some questioning, Ellie said that she couldn't allow herself to have fun because the week had been slow and she hadn't *earned* her free time.

Marge had a week off from work and was having trouble controlling her binge eating. It had been raining hard, and she stayed indoors feeling locked in and frustrated. She spent one whole day cleaning her house from top to bottom. This activity gave her a good feeling, and she didn't think about food all day. But when the cleaning was done, she became fearful of the lure of the kitchen. She remembered that her mother used to say, "Idle hands are the devil's playthings." Marge could allow herself to clean the house and to read mind-improving books for fun but not "frivolous" novels. Both Marge and Ellie had to *earn* free time and *use* it productively.

Perfectionistic binge eaters seem to think that setting the highest possible standards will result in achieving these goals and also achieving satisfaction. This is not the case. The more you pressure yourself, the harder it becomes to relax and get on with your project.

Many individuals are afraid of setting lower goals because they think they need the motivation of prodding and pressure. Setting a lower goals gives you the opportunity to surpass it. In my compulsivity classes, I had the participants make self-contracts. Each person set a weight loss goal for the eight weeks of classes. Although in Lesson One I urged them all to set surefire goals that they knew they could achieve no matter what, most did not listen and set themselves unreasonable challenges. On the last day of class, I asked each person to share what that goal was and

126

whether it had been achieved. Many students reported losses of ten or twelve pounds. Most members of the class were happy and smiling. When it was Lois's turn, she replied with tears in her eyes that she had not achieved her goal. She was ashamed because her eight-week goal was to lose twenty pounds and she had lost only eighteen! If Lois had set her goal at ten or twelve pounds, she would have felt ecstatic at her eighteen-pound loss, but she set herself up for bad feelings by insisting that she *should* lose twenty pounds and therefore would lose it all in eight weeks.

The perfectionist binge eater will block her progress at every turn if she expects immediate and complete change. Instead of seeing the process as one of evolution (change through baby steps and small successes), the perfectionist, echoing the demands of her parents, will judge herself a loser and shop from diet to diet and doctor to doctor, testing each one and herself, but never accomplishing her goal because she continues to act unloving and unreasonable toward herself.

When the perfectionist risks being less than perfect, allowing herself to do her best and accepting that, she will begin to see results—and ultimately she will be a winner.

SEXUALITY AND BINGE EATING

The person with an eating disorder is usually under the impression that unless she looks a certain way, she is not attractive. The majority of anorectics, bulimics, and compulsive overeaters *are women who have given men the power to tell them that they are lovable*. Again, *lovable*

127

means thin. Although many of the women I have treated are career women who are capable and intelligent, they think that they are nothing without a man. The men they love, or seek to love, don't have to be good-looking or perfect in any way, but to qualify to be a partner to this desirable man, the woman must live by a different standard of excellence.

Elaine was tearful because she had been working very hard to lose the fifty pounds she had gained after she had given up her dependence on alcohol. In the past, she had always been very slim. She realized that the fifty pounds represented all the hurt and fear that she had kept inside while she was drinking. Now she was free of alcohol and determined to put her life in order.

The tears were because her husband had suggested, after seeing a movie on TV, that Elaine consider breast augmentation so she would look like one of the luscious leading ladies in the film. Elaine was hurt and angry. She wanted to be loved for herself and not as a body, an object to be molded like a statue. She feared that no matter how much weight she lost, her husband still would find her unattractive and undesirable.

Elaine's story is not uncommon. Many women, both average and overweight, worry about what their men want them to look like. Yet very few women ever tell their male partners that they are unlovable because they have fat rumps or beer bellies. Women tend to be accepting of the bodies of the men they love. Although some spouses and lovers are accepting of the bodies of their wives and girl friends, the food addict often refuses to allow herself to be accepted because she is judging herself against her fantasy of beauty.

A woman once told me her husband said that he was never aware when she had gained a few pounds by looking at her, but he could tell her weight was up because she moved differently. She hated herself and gave out nonverbal messages about her unattractiveness. Any number of women also push away the sexual advances of their mates because they feel ugly and don't believe that a male could find them desirable. Some spouses reinforce this negative value by turning away and cutting down on sex.

SEX ROLES AND WOMEN'S LIBERATION

There are two aspects of the sexual issue for people who are binge eaters: sex roles and sexuality. Sex roles have been influenced by the women's movement. More women are competing with men in the work world and thinking of themselves as equals. They are doing as good a job as men but are still being underpaid and undervalued, often treated as empty-headed dolls. Many women, especially single mothers, are caught in the conflict of thinking they are betraying their children by not being homebound housewives and mothers while, at the same time, wanting to expand themselves as talented and creative workers. Sexual harassment is another growing problem for women. A liberated young woman who works as an electrician is on leave at present because she could not deal with the sexual remarks and threats of the men with whom she worked.

Liz was attending law school and working as a secretary. She was searching for a new job and called about an ad in the paper. The man who answered the phone asked her what her qualifications were and what she looked like. She asked why he wanted to know about her looks, and he replied, "I interviewed someone yesterday for the job. She was highly qualified, but she weighed 180 pounds. What do you look like?" Liz told him that she didn't want a job based on her measurements.

Roles are changing; men are sometimes house-husbands while their wives support the family. The economy makes it imperative for many married women to work. A young woman about to graduate from college explained that she had finally realized that her old dream to graduate, get married and be taken care of was shattered for good. She knew that she probably would have to work for a good portion of her life and that the chances of divorce were very high for everyone in her age group. She decided to stop thinking of herself as a "princess" and get on with the happy chore of finding out who she really was and what her potential was for having a satisfying career, not just a job.

Some overweight women use their fat as a statement: "See through this fat to the real person I am, and then I will trust you." This attitude is like the fairy tale of the princess on the glass mountain. Only the young man brave enough and resourceful enough to scale the mountain will win the hand of the princess. Fat can be that mountain.

The woman of today needs to rethink her role in society. Those who become professionals or career women must battle to earn as much as men and be valued for their abilities, not their looks. There is a conflict between the desire to look beautiful enough to attract a mate and that wish to be OK no matter what. One woman who lost weight, had a nose job, and had the "cellulite" removed from her thighs still did not feel good-looking enough to believe her husband's compliments were sincere. She hated herself before, and she couldn't accept who she now was. She was stuck.

In a discussion with a group of overweight housewives, the idea of fat giving a person a look of strength was shared. Some of the women felt big when they were overweight. "Big" and "strong" are synonymous for them. They had large families and needed strength and stamina to do the chores and cope with family problems.

Many overweight binge eaters believe that fat is a protection. Jennie was a lawyer and very eager to get ahead. She knew that she feared that if she were thin she would be expected to meet someone and get married. Her fantasy about marriage was that of her parents' marriage, in which the woman stayed home and raised children while the man was the professional. Until she rewrote her script to allow herself to enjoy both career and a loving relationship she could not lose weight and keep it off.

SEX, LOVE AND FOOD

Sexuality is always an issue in binge eating. Anorectics seem to deny their sexuality and are usually not sexually active. As they starve, their bodies become more and more lethargic and sexual desire disappears. The anorectic's goal is to appear asexual and stick-thin. Along with anorexia often go infertility and cessation of the menstrual cycle.

Bulimics, on the other hand, seem to be much more active and even promiscuous in their sexual lives. Because of the intensity of the binge/purge compulsion and the feelings of self-abnegation, bulimics isolate themselves from loved ones through secrecy. Many of the bulimic women I treat are married but have never told their husbands of their long-standing eating problem. How does a relationship succeed when there is secrecy and lack of intimacy and trust? Often the fear of his judgment keeps her from loving her mate. She must play the role of the beautiful, understanding, "together" person at all costs.

Since family counseling often hastens the recovery from binge eating, I am sometimes able to persuade the food abuser to bring in her spouse or lover. Usually the husband is shocked and amazed at how little he knows about his wife——her fears, her great self-doubt, and her obsession with food. It is as if he were living with a stranger. When he offers his assistance and willingness to understand his wife in more realistic terms, some of her self-imposed burden of perfection is lifted and she is freed from the anxiety that surrounds her need for secrecy.

Many bulimics separate love and sex. They are able to get physical needs met through "one-night stands" or casual relationships but fear a long-term commitment.

Tammy has been married twice. She told me that her father becomes very distant and critical of her when she is married but is warm and intimate when she is between relationships. Another woman who is torn between her father and a lover is Veronica. Veronica has only casual sex. When she is attracted to someone she keeps herself distant because she is afraid that her father would find her in bed with the man and be angry.

People with eating disorders experience a spectrum of behavior relating to sexuality that ranges from lack of interest in sex and in themselves as sexual people to healthy sexual behavior to promiscuity. Feelings of self-loathing lead to fears of accepting one's sexuality. Many binge eaters are afraid of calling attention to themselves. They are afraid of their sexual nature yet are caught in their sexual urges. Binging can easily replace sex for some of these people.

Avodah Offit, M.D., a sex therapist, talks about the relationship between eating and sex in her book *Night Thoughts: Reflections of a Sex Therapist*:

> The act of eating, then, consists of desire with salivation, the excitement of tasting and chewing, and the orgasmic contractions of swallowing, repeated again and again. No physical act we perform is so like sexual union. People eat compulsively to excess in order to distract themselves pleasurably from pain. While busy chewing and eating and thinking of food, they have little room in their psyches for sexual longings, for fears of intimacy, self-assertion, and dependence, or for anger and grief. They swallow and reach, swallow and reach.

Fears of being intimate abound among compulsive bingers who are afraid of revealing themselves as flawed people. Overcoming food abuse requires a new way of thinking and feeling as well as behaving. The binge eater must work to love herself and think of herself as lovable and desirable no matter what others think. When she begins to like herself, she will see others as her equals, not her superiors. Owning her body means owning her femininity as a sexual being.

III

*A Self-Help Program
for Change*

THE FOUR-LEVEL PLAN: AN OVERVIEW

To overcome the problem of compulsive binging, purging, or starving permanently, a four-level plan must be put into effect. This plan is multidimensional, involving change on the physical, intellectual, emotional, and spiritual levels. I call the last level the transpersonal or inner power aspect of change.

I used to think that behavior modification alone was all that was necessary to end the problems of eating disorders. Yet self-monitored eating plans and awareness of the social situations or emotions that trigger binges proved not to be enough. As soon as the individual experienced a crisis or significant change in her life, she often reverted to old behaviors and, in the case of compulsive overeaters, soon gained back all her weight. In addition, the issue of resistance kept cropping up. Many students rationalized why they could not or would not make a commitment to alter their eating behavior.

Some food abusers have been in conventional psychotherapy and reported that the experience greatly improved the quality of their lives, but they had not overcome compulsive binging or purging nor had they managed to lose weight.

Binge eaters have often told me that they have been assured by doctors or therapists that the binge behavior would disappear on its own while they worked on the underlying problems. I recall a woman recovering from a divorce whose therapist told her that it was all right to continue binging while they worked on the more important areas. The therapist ignored the fact (that I have discovered) that binge eating is, in itself, a key to exploring emotional upheavals and can be used in learning to gain new insights and techniques for change.

Since the majority of food abusers are not conscious of the connection between emotions and overeating, I have discovered that to learn how to stop binging, one has to work backwards from the overt behavior of the binge or purge to the root cause: the person's thought system. The four-level plan teaches the food addict to acknowledge her eating behavior and become willing to understand the misuse of food without judgment, to look for the intense feelings that trigger the binge, to reach for the underlying thoughts or beliefs that give rise to those feelings, and to take action to avoid further anxiety and subsequent compulsive episodes.

This is how I work with a client. Step one is an examination of her eating history by keeping a food diary for a week. This food diary shows what, how much and when she ate. We discuss each episode of overeating or purging and look for the feelings that particular binge was camouflaging. That discussion is step two.

For instance, Paula binged all day Sunday but could not figure out why she did it. Her food intake the previous day was normal and healthy. She had had a wonderful Saturday working on a hobby and spending time with her husband and baby. What happened between Saturday and Sunday? "Oh yes," she said, "I was up four times during the night with my baby. She has been waking every night for a month, and I am totally exhausted." Then she revealed that the feelings behind her binge behavior were both physical and emotional. Physically, she was worn out from enduring a month of semisleepless nights. Emotionally, she was angry for having to get up, and she was annoyed with her husband for not being helpful or supportive about taking care of the baby.

Behind every binge is an intense emotion, either positive or negative, that is uncomfortable to the binge eater. It may take a little practice to learn to uncover that emotion.

The third step is to go beyond the experience of emotion to the thought or idea that fostered that particular feeling. Paula believed that marriage meant having children. She also believed that a husband should be excited and eager to help raise and care for the children in ways other than just earning money to support the family. Another common belief that led Paula straight to the refrigerator was, "I'm tired. If I eat something I will feel better." So, at 3:00 A.M. she made a beeline for the kitchen because she was exhausted and feeling let down by her husband.

The fourth step is the most vital part of the plan: to retrieve your inner power to change your thoughts or solve your problem. Paula decided to ask her husband to help her by taking turns getting up with the baby. She also asked him to baby-sit more often so she could have a block of time to use for herself. She then felt less tired and less resentful.

To know and use your own personal power, your may need to learn new techniques such as journal writing, meditation, consciousness-raising, dream analysis, or positive self-affirmation. Classes, support groups, or individual counseling may be convenient sources for learning some of these skills.

When you work on changing only one aspect of yourself such as your body through diet, fasting, or behavioral training, you will achieve only partial success. Most binge eaters are so obsessed with the desire to be perfect and look beautiful that they frequently tell themselves they would rather die than be ugly or fat. It may be hard for you to realize that you are more than just a body. Part of the recovery from eating disorders is to learn to see yourself from a new perspective and learn to integrate all the parts of your being into a lovable and capable whole, not just a body that acts as a clothes hanger.

LEVEL 1: PHYSICAL OR BEHAVIORAL CHANGE

The four-level plan starts with physical change or behavioral training, because all binge eaters are basically interested in eliminating the binge or binge/purge problem. The majority of binge eaters believe that when the symptom goes away, they are cured. Unfortunately, this is usually not the case. Unless there are changes in life-style, belief systems, and problem-solving skills together with improvement in self-image and stress reduction, the symptom may return during times of anxiety.

An examination of eating behavior is the easiest place for a binge eater to start for, of course, she is intimately involved with her binge episodes and is obsessed by thoughts of food. Changing the food intake may have an effect on the physical well-being of the person. Changing certain parts of the diet, reducing the consumption of sugar- or salt-laden foods can alleviate some depression caused by the discomfort of bloating or the "spaced-out" feelings that come with intense binging or binge/purge aftermath. Choosing to eat foods that you usually forbid yourself and learning to eat them in moderation will eliminate feelings of deprivation that often lead to binges.

Physical or behavioral change involves two steps. First, the binge eater must confide her problem to a professional. Bulimics and anorectics need to have a physical checkup to pinpoint medical problems that are interfering with their health. Sometimes, when chemical imbalances are brought under control, the depressed state will lighten and they will feel more excited and happy about pursuing a new way of eating.

The second step on the level of physical change involves behavior modification, starting with a re-evaluation of the binge eater's eating habits and preferences. Next, the binge eater must confront and "own" (be responsible for) her behavior around food. She must learn to eliminate self-condemning judgment about her eating binges. A food diary is essential to achieve a sense of awareness of the behavior and to learn to take responsibility for that behavior.

Behavioral change also involves making new choices about what to eat and how much to eat. Learning how to handle eating situations that provoke anxiety, such as buffets, dinner with your parents, weddings, or even a meal in a restaurant with friends, is a positive step. The most important aspect of behavior change involves new thinking and feeling about food in order to become free of the bondage of diets. How each person behaves is also a direct result of how she reacts to her life situation.

Valerie is a case in point. She had stopped purging for more than six months but still had occasional binges. Valerie was concerned because although her binges had become infrequent, when she did eat compulsively, it seemed worse than before. Her binges were rare because she was not dealing with most of the stress and conflict in her life in a healthy and productive way. She had learned to assert herself, to communicate better with her fellow workers and friends, to give herself permission to have better relationships, and she was having more fun. She no longer felt like a victim of fate.

The binges she still experienced were intense because they reflected the core issues yet to be faced and solved. If Valerie's daily life could be measured on a scale of 1 to 10 with 10 being huge internal earthquakes, I would say that she had conquered the problems that were unpleasant up to 6.9 on her Richter scale. Valerie still has to face her tendency to put herself down and her doubt that others will accept her unless she is perfect. Basic issues of self-esteem and Valerie's inability to maintain a warm and loving intimate relationship with a man resonate on a scale of 8, 9, and 10. These are the emotional tremors that still unnerve her. That's why her binges are in the 8 and 9 range of intensity.

In time, these binges will disappear as she resolves her feelings about herself and her interpersonal relationships and becomes aware, before a binge, of what she is reacting to.

LEVEL 2: EMOTIONAL CHANGE

Emotional change is essential to recover from binge eating. A binge is a cover-up and tells you that you are not being honest with yourself about your feelings or the intensity of your emotions. You may be denying negative emotions such as anger, guilt, fear, and hurt. Perhaps you are trying to talk yourself out of your resentment through self-discount—a process in which you do not give yourself permission to feel anything negative because you believe that it is bad or people won't like you. The result of self-discount is that you keep yourself a victim, continue to feel helpless, and rage at your helplessness.

Vera was used to eating handfuls of nuts throughout the day at her job (which she hates), blaming her nibbling on the fact that a bowl of nuts is always available near the water cooler, and she must pass it frequently. She could decide to remove the nuts, fill the bowl with sugarless gum, or leave the nuts and learn to say "no" to them. I asked her first to continue to reach for the nuts in order to assess her mood during the day and to find out how anxious or unhappy she was. Once she could see that her day-long nibbling was like popping tranquilizers to keep herself calm, she could decide whether the real problem was the food or her unhappiness in a dead-end job. This would lead to action for change in both areas and away from continued helplessness and food abuse.

A majority of food abusers seem to do most of their eating or purging in the evening or night. Binge eaters can fill the daytime hours with jobs, chores, or activities that keep them from feeling or thinking too much. But in the evening, when the day's schedule calms down, the thoughts and feelings come flowing in like the tide. For some it is a tidal wave. The evening hours may be too lonely for some. For others, the quiet brings time for reflection on frustration about being hard-pressed for money, working nine to five at a hateful job, or being cooped up at night with an unresponsive spouse. I once knew a woman who was able to fill her evenings with fascinating activities, hobbies, social events and classes. The only nights she binged were the two evenings she forced herself to stay home with her husband. He watched TV or read, not talking to her or showing her attention, so she ate to block out her angry feelings.

Start by accepting the idea that a binge is an explosion of emotion. Then practice being in touch with feelings, knowing what feelings are, and relating feelings to situations or relationships. By postponing the onset of a binge, the food addict can get in touch with the feeling that is driving her to want food. She is then learning to interrupt the cycle of the binge and is on the road to recovery.

I have worked with some individuals who have had previous psychotherapy and are able to tune in to their emotions with ease. Some of these people are stuck in the feeling state and act as if the feelings were facts. Thus intense fear or guilt will paralyze them as they tell themselves, "Something terrible will happen" or "It's all my fault." Often feelings are a result of one's fantasies or fears and are not the truth. To free oneself from being a slave of emotional feelings, the third level of the four-level plan—intellectual change—must be introduced.

LEVEL 3: INTELLECTUAL CHANGE

Intellectual change focuses on the beliefs or ideas that you have and on the things you tell yourself about food and about who you are, every minute of the day. Your thoughts and beliefs influence your feelings. It is common in Overeaters Anonymous for each speaker to introduce herself by saying, "I'm Jane, compulsive overeater." A very wise woman who pondered the outcome of constantly labeling herself as a person with a problem, changed her greeting to "I'm Mary, committed abstainer." She meant that she wanted to overcome her problem of binge eating and label herself as someone committed to the idea of abstinence from compulsive overeating. This is an example of how changing your beliefs can alter your behavior. If Mary continued to see herself as a person who had and would always have a problem, she would continue to feel like a "loser" and a second-class citizen. By affirming her goal to stop binge eating and be in charge of her behavior, she propelled herself to a place of power. Mary transcended her problem. She gave up compulsive eating and lived life as a healthy and capable person.

Give yourself new watchwords and self-descriptions, and you will feel different and act differently. Instead of saying, "When I eat one apple I am OK, but two apples equal a binge, so I might as well keep eating," you can learn to tell yourself, "Two apples are only two apples. I can stop eating now." People commonly say, "I'm a chocoholic." In so saying you are giving yourself permission to overeat chocolate (which means you can also have permission to "undereat" chocolate).

During the first meeting of a behavior modification class, a woman challenged me to teach her how to each just one piece of pizza and stop. She told the class that she couldn't control herself when she was faced with pizza. The second week she announced that she was still afraid of pizza but had eaten one potato chip and stopped. A gasp of amazement was heard around the room. If she could eat one chip and stop, she could certainly learn to eat one piece of pizza and stop. The problem was all in her mind. By the eighth week, she had changed her thinking and changed her behavior so that she did indeed eat just one piece of pizza and stop without feeling deprived.

Understanding the interrelationship between your behavior, feelings, and thoughts will lead to dramatic change. By practicing awareness techniques and skills in listening to your inner dialogue and changing it, you will be able to be your own therapist. There is, however, another level to this plan of overall change.

LEVEL 4: TRANSPERSONAL LEVEL

The fourth level is the transpersonal level, the level of personal power. The term transpersonal refers to all the undiscovered capacities you are unaware of that are beyond the limitations set by your self-concept. This level lies just beyond the growing edge of self-awareness. Another way of thinking about it is that you are more than you think you are. What you think about yourself is not always the truth and can severely limit you.

One tool of the transpersonal level is the power of faith or spiritual belief. For those who use prayer or meditation, this level will help you employ your spirituality in order to change. Relying on a higher power as in the Overeaters Anonymous twelve-step program brings dramatic results for many. Some individuals like to read uplifting books, attend church, or learn how to meditate.

There is a creative unconscious within each human being which can be used as an ally to aid and abet you in your search for health and happiness. You can learn to get in touch with this special inner self through journal writing, guided imagery, art, and music as well as dream interpretation. Exploring the transpersonal level may be a new and wonderful adventure for a person who is caught up in the belief that she has an insurmountable problem.

The transpersonal level provided an experience for Carla that helped her make a sudden and positive change in her binge behavior. Carla's father had died fifteen years earlier. She had begun compulsive eating on a grand scale at that time and had not been able to overcome her problem, even though she was intelligent, self-aware, determined, and thought she had tried everything.

Carla had become so ill when her father died that she had not been able to participate in the rituals of mourning and had held on to her grief for fifteen years. During a guided imagery session, she fantasized a visit with her father. In her fantasy, she was able to express her grief and become aware that when her father died no one was left in her life to give her the love he had given her. So she had decided to fill the void with food. She ended her mourning and received assurance from the spirit of her father that it was time to get on with her life and fill that void with love from others. After the session, Carla experienced very little trouble in staying on a diet program to lose weight. She found herself filled with new ideas and energy and began looking into a retraining program to enter a career that she had always longed to have but never allowed herself to pursue.

The four-level plan is a program that will help food addicts to understand the dynamics of their compulsive behavior and to make the changes necessary for permanent health. The program I have invented is simple but not always easy. There are only four basic steps to follow:

1. Evaluate your eating behavior and the foods you choose for binges or emotional eating episodes. Rate each episode on a scale of 1 to 10 (with 10 being the most intense).
2. Name the feelings that triggered the eating episode. What situation or relationship is involved?
3. Discover what thoughts or beliefs about this situation or relationship led to the intense feelings.
4. Retrieve your inner power; recognize that you are not helpless. Decide on appropriate action. (Use your positive qualities to change what you think or change the troublesome situation.)

You will soon make a habit of examining your food diary in an impartial way and acting like a detective to trace a binge to the feeling that precipitated it and then to the source of the emotion—the thought. In time you will make friends with your inner power and gain access to those qualities and powers that have always been available to your but of which you were not aware.

CHANGING WHAT YOU DO

The aftermath of a binge is usually self-hatred and a desire to blot out the unhappy episode. If you sweep your binges under the rug of your consciousness, you will never learn how to stop. The hardest part of changing your behavior is to decide to become aware of it and accept responsibility for it.

When a food addict comes to me with the sole goal of losing weight, I explain that the process is twofold: first, to understand the eating behavior (amounts, type of foods, frequency of eating, and so on), and second, to make decisions to change the intake in order to lose weight. People who start with the second step will most likely have only temporary success. To impose an eating plan artificially on a person who is an emotional eater is to plug up a volcano. It will erupt sooner or later.

III: A Self-Help Program for Change

WHAT IS A FOOD DIARY?

The first step is to collect information about the person's behavior with food. This is done by keeping track of what the individual eats and drinks each day. It is called a food diary or food journal and is an ongoing record of daily food behavior, experiences, and thoughts.

The food diary is the central tool for the beginning of self-awareness. If you write down what you eat, you will know what you are doing. If you don't, you will perpetuate delusions and inappropriate eating. To write down your food intake at the end of the day or end of the week is a waste of time. You need to keep track as you go. The food diary is not a report card! It is not a paper that reveals that you are good or bad. It is raw data! You can't solve your problem unless you have the basic facts to work from. The food diary is like a graph. It will reflect what is going on in your life day by day. You will notice that changes in your eating habits or binges reflect both happy and upsetting situations in your life.

Some people write down only the "good" days or "good" meals. This shows immediately that they have a strongly developed "diet master" conscience. I remind you again that the food diary is not a judgment sheet but a much needed record of your behavior. You will learn more from the "bad" days than the "good" ones. Once you get past your reluctance to look at what you are consuming, you have made headway. Most bingers do not want to be responsible for their choices. Some complain that keeping a food diary spoils the spontaneity of eating. This is an excuse. If you are not ready to take this first step you will have very poor results in your endeavors to end your problem.

All food abusers live in a world of fantasy. They tell themselves that food eaten on the way to the sink doesn't count. They either minimize or maximize the calories consumed. Some will look at a serving of ice cream and tell themselves they are pigs, consuming 500 calories, when a usual scoop is 150. One woman I know forbids herself bread in any form. She has decided that bread is an extravagance of calories. The average slice contains 75 calories. Binge eaters are also prone to suffer from food amnesia. They think they remember what they have eaten all day but frequently forget the roll or cookies at 3:00 P.M.

There are many variations of food diaries. Some behavior modification classes hand out very extensive sheets asking you to rate your hunger, note in what room in the house you tend to eat, who you are with, what you eat, and how you feel. Many of my clients have designed their own sheets. They should include the date and time of eating, names of foods, either quantities or calories eaten, and thoughts or feelings they had at that time. For bulimics, it is imperative to note the food that is purged as well as the food that is assimilated.

Some food addicts have small, healthy meals during the day but large binges at night. For these people the primary focus may be on the binge episodes. I suggest recording the foods eaten, the amounts, and the emotional intensity on a scale of 1 to 10. Thoughts or insights may be written later because most people in the midst of a binge are disoriented or unwilling to confront the experience immediately. Whether you choose a small notebook or a printed food journal sheet, *write down your food intake*!

What do you do if you record for one or two days and then skip and feel so guilty that you don't go back to the diary because you "blew it" by skipping days? Start by asking yourself a few simple questions that will help you make a commitment to yourself that is *loving* and *reasonable*:

1. Am I willing to keep a food diary?
2. What kind of recordkeeping am I willing to do? Am I willing only to write down the names of foods and not the amounts of calories? Am I willing to write down amounts but not calories? Am I willing to write down both the names of foods and calories?
3. How many days will I *really* keep my promise to myself to keep a food diary?

Please be aware that you may be asking yourself how many days the experts expect you to write down your food—seven days every week. That is not what I asked. The question is: In your heart of hearts—how many days will you do it?

Start with where you are, not where you think you should be or where your doctor or nutritionist thinks you should be. If you write down four days' worth of food a week but sternly mandate seven days, you will feel like a washout. Go over the questions again. Be brutally honest with yourself. You may be willing to write down only the names of the foods you eat and only one day this week. *Wonderful!!* Now do it! Each week you can make a new commitment. Accept yourself as you are today and let yourself do a less-than-perfect job as long as you make a beginning. Perhaps next week you will commit yourself only to one day again, but the following week you may know that you can handle three days. Write what you are willing to write, but keep writing down what you are eating and drinking.

It is difficult for the food addict to read his or her food diary in an objective manner. You may tend to judge yourself as "bad" for overeating or purging on certain days. The food diary has vital information for you. Perhaps you have a friend you can trust enough to share your eating record with. If you have a therapist, she will surely be willing to help you. See if you can reread your list with new eyes. Here are some questions that may help you:

1. How many calories did you consume overall this week and/or each day?
2. Is each day the same in pattern and amounts of eating? What days are different? How are they different? What was happening on the days that were out of sync?
3. Are the weekends different from weekdays? What are the differences? What is different about Saturday and/or Sunday for you?
4. What foods did you eat over and over? Were they "diet" foods? If so, did you eat them because you really wanted them, because you thought you should, or because they filled you up? If the foods you ate over and over were high in calories or salt, why did you choose them?
5. What size portions did you eat? Looking back on it, how do you feel about the portions?

6. Were there any days or times of day that were more stressful for you? Was this feeling the same every day or just occasionally during the week? (Some people find that evenings are the hardest; others have trouble during lunchtime or coffee break.)

7. Did you feel upset or anxious about any people in your life? What days or times did this occur? Look at your food intake for that day. What does it tell you?

8. Did you allow yourself to have any foods that you love and consider a "no-no"? How often did you choose to eat *one* portion and stop? Can you remember how you felt? Did you feel powerful and in control? Did you feel "normal"? Did you feel scared? Did it lead to an overeating episode or purge?

9. Looking over the entire list, rate your choices objectively for good nutritional balance. Did you include foods from the major food groups? What suggestions would you offer if this were someone else's food diary?

10. Are you taking nutritional supplements? Do you think they are helpful? Would you want to take vitamins or minerals to aid in assuring your well-being? Do you know how to tell if you need or don't need vitamins?

THE BINGE RATING SYSTEM

The food diary will show you when you are eating emotionally. Many bingers are not able to tune in to the intensity of their feelings. I have, therefore, devised a system to help you learn how to link your food intake to the experiences of your life. I call it the Binge Rating System.

Here is what you do. Most people have heard of the Richter scale that measures geologic earthquakes on a scale of 1 to 10. Some tremors register 4.5, others 6.8 or 8.2.

1. Read over your food diary for the day. Look for episodes of overeating or binging.
2. Rate the eating experience as if it were a quake. Use the scale of 1 to 10.
3. Ask yourself what happened in the last twenty-four hours that corresponds to that earthquake rating.

Beryl had had a wonderful week. But she binged on Sunday and could not find the reason. That day she and her family had gone to Disneyland. It was a time of fun. Why did Beryl have a binge when she came home? I asked her to rate her binge. She rated it 6.3.

Beryl began to think about her day at Disneyland and searched her memory for any discomfort. She recalled that at Disneyland her children and husband had been snacking and enjoying some of the fast-food treats that were available. Beryl was a vegetarian. She could find little to eat at Disneyland. Each food she bought was unsatisfactory. It either tasted bad or was not what she really wanted. By the end of the day she felt extremely deprived. The "little girl" side of Beryl was jealous of her children having all the goodies they wanted. She made up for it when she got home.

Claudia rated her nighttime binge as a 9.5. She had attended a family dinner party. In front of all the assembled guests, her uncle had told her she shouldn't eat dessert because she was too fat. Claudia was embarrassed and very, very angry. She was not able to express her hurt to her uncle so she "ate at him." Claudia is very nonassertive. She rarely expresses anger. Now she can see by the intensity of her binges just how much emotion she is suppressing.

Rating your eating experience by its intensity rather than quantity consumed may enable you to understand yourself better. If you rate a binge by the quality of food consumed, with 2,000 calories being the low end, many binges would be inconsequential. Each binge eater must have the freedom to evaluate her own performance. Many bingers do not eat large quantities—they eat different types of food when they binge. For a woman who is allergic or hypoglycemic, eating four cookies is a real temper tantrum because these foods might make her ill and are forbidden.

Even if you are resistant to keeping a daily food diary, you may find that rating your eating behavior every day at the end of the day can be an interesting and useful experience. You can plan a few minutes of daily review in which you ask yourself three easy questions:

Daily Review

- How do I rate my eating for today on an emotional scale of 1 to 10?
- What was the emotional equivalent of that rating in terms of situations and relationships in my life?

- How can I stop feeling like a victim and do something to change the situation I am reacting to?

STOP DIETING

Another way to change what you are doing is to stop dieting. I have already discussed why diets don't work. Dieters feel deprived all the time. Deprivation leads to binging. Binging leads to harsher dieting. It is a vicious circle and a destructive behavioral cycle.

If you are used to judging foods as good or bad depending on whether they are allowed on all the diets you have even been on, you are on the wrong track. Hundreds of people in my classes have succeeded in either controlling their binges or losing weight simply by counting calories, and they didn't have to give up foods that they like. Most behavior modification programs teach you to make your own choices about what you eat. You can make sure that you don't overeat by counting calories. This approach helps you to limit your intake so that you can eat what you want. Calorie counting helps you to learn what a moderate portion really is.

Another plus for nondieting is that you can learn to have some of the foods that you usually forbid yourself and not gain weight. When you have some ice cream or bread every day or a few times a week, the overwhelming craving disappears. You don't have to eat a whole loaf if you know that tomorrow you can have some of that food again.

Many long-time binge eaters, anorectics, bulimics, and obese compulsive eaters complain that they must eat less

159

than 1,000 calories or they will gain weight. Overweight individuals who have dieted for years tell me that they can lose weight only if they eat less than 700 calories. This hopeless situation has arisen because the body has learned to accommodate the small intake of food over the years of extreme behavior and dieting by changing the metabolism. The body burns up the ingested food more and more slowly. Eventually, the person finds herself limited to a lifetime of eating 700 calories per day just to maintain her weight.

For these people, it is important to learn how to increase the amount of food to a healthy level and to accept these larger amounts without telling themselves that they are on a binge. Bulimics are so afraid of gaining weight that even a tiny increase is often resisted. The food diary is useful for helping people learn to make new choices and gradually to build up the body's tolerance for increased calories.

Since many binges result from nutritional starvation, accurate and honest recordkeeping will help the fearful food addict eliminate many binge episodes when she begins to eat foods from the major food groups that fulfill her body's needs. Counseling can aid her in controlling the panic and fearful thoughts such as that eating a piece of bread will automatically result in a weight gain.

The key to change is *consciousness*. Stan has spent the last five years binging and fasting. He is a walking calculator. He knows the calorie and nutritional content of most foods, but he has brainwashed himself into thinking that certain foods are "bad," diet-breakers, or will "set him off" so he can't eat just a little. He has built up an attitude toward food and a way of eating that stresses very low-cal diet foods. This keeps him feeling deprived and ensures periodic extremes of binging on ultra-high-calorie food. I persuaded Stan that he could easily stop this seesaw approach to food if he would be willing to suspend his judgment about foods and simply eat what he wanted, using a calorie-counting approach to control his intake. *He was forbidden to diet.* I explained that there were no good or bad foods, only the foods he chose to eat. We agreed that he could eat as much as 2,000 calories a day.

Miracle of miracles, Stan discovered that he was not even averaging 2,000 calories a day. He was eating what he wanted when he was hungry. The trick was in writing it down on paper as he went along; he could then see the *truth* about his behavior. He was amazed to find that when he ate what he liked, he felt extremely satisfied. He also discovered something that many others have learned: that he really doesn't like food all that much. His favorite food, frozen yogurt, could easily be worked into his food choices every day at 200 calories per portion. Stan confided to me that now he knows what it feels like to be a normal eater. He used to be very thin but was constantly obsessed with thoughts of food and diets. Now he is still slim but feels free around food.

When you stop dieting and learn to give up your fear of food, you can enjoy learning how to manage your calories. Keeping a food diary may seem like a burden, but it doesn't have to last forever. Keep your food diary until you understand—until you stop lying to yourself. When you behave responsibly around food, you have internalized the information. You no longer need to keep a food diary when you know what "moderate" means, when you don't eat when you aren't hungry, and when you no longer feel guilty about eating. Until that time, however, your food diary is training you by showing you what you are eating, how much, and when. By using this information, you can begin to rethink your choices.

When you go shopping for clothing do you buy *anything* and *everything* you want without looking at the price tag? Most of us do look at the price tag, whether it be on a dress, a TV, or a car. We ask ourselves two questions before purchasing the item:

1. Is this item worth the price? (Am I getting my money's worth?)
2. Can I afford this item?

You can learn to choose foods the same way.

The important thing in keeping a food diary is to keep asking yourself if a specific food is really "worth it" to you. If it is, don't worry about what others think, have it. But remember to ask yourself if you can afford it.

I recognize that there are many credit-card bingers. One client told me that after she gave up overeating, and was angry with her husband, she began to "spend at him" instead. She would go shopping and charge things in a buying binge to get even with him.

If you write down what you choose to eat as you go along, you will see what is left in your calorie balance. Knowing your resources will help you figure out how best to spend your allotment of calories.

Some people have made a game of counting calories. Here are two methods invented by some of my clients:

1. Use play money and give yourself an allowance every day, which you pay out.
2. Use the check register that comes with your checkbook and subtract as you spend the calories.

The food diary will also inform you about the specific foods that you are using symbolically. Some of the phrases I have heard from food abusers are: "I was so angry, I ate all the nuts." "When I'm sick, I like baby food." (Baby food here means soft things like hot cereal, rice, and mashed potatoes—not actual baby food.) And "Sweets are love and make things seem nice."

Time after time I see food diaries filled with days of fresh vegetables, fish or chicken, and some fruit interspersed with binges of chocolate, bread, and junk food. The all-or-nothing approach to eating leads to intensive binges. When you stop dieting and allow yourself to believe that there are no bad foods, you will be able to take the good/bad labels off some of the foods you binge on. When a food loses its allure, it doesn't beckon as strongly.

There is also a group of overeaters who do not have gigantic binges but seem to eat constantly throughout the day. Their snack choices are usually high-calorie sweets or junk foods. I call this "tranquilizer eating." The compulsive eater is dropping food into her system to maintain an even level of "comfort" and keep the anxiety at bay.

Finally, the food diary can help the average foodaholic who long ago lost touch with feelings of hunger and satiety. Counting calories can help this person to become aware of the inner workings of the digestive tract. Eating limited portions slowly can enable the binge eater to feel satisfied and full on less food than she ever thought possible. That is because the stomach holds only about two cups of food. It takes about twenty minutes for the brain to receive the message that the stomach is full, so eating slowly will ensure that you do not overfill your stomach. Anyone can learn to slow down and eat smaller bites of food.

MAKE NEW CHOICES

Many of people with eating disorders gave up control over their choice of what foods to eat when they were children. They gave that power to their parents. For those people, knowing what to eat is sometimes hit or miss.

A lifetime of dieting also instills a fear of eating what you really want. For people who have spent years denying their food preferences and suppressing their desires so they could stay on a diet, I offer a short quiz that I call "To Thine Own Self Be True." When you want something but you don't know what you want, or you do know what you want but tell yourself that it is bad, follow these steps. Do this before you open the refrigerator or before you leave the house for a dinner at a restaurant. Take one minute and answer these questions:

- How hungry am I?
- Do I want something to eat or something to drink?
- Do I want a "heavy" food or a "light" food?
- Do I want hot food or cold food?
- Do I want something, smooth, crunchy, spongy, chewy?
- Do I want something sweet, salty, sour, spicy?

You will discover the kind of food experience you find most satisfying. You may not know the name of the food you want, but you may find that you want something sweet. What is the texture of the sweet food you want? By taking time to think out your desires, you will be able to find out exactly what will satisfy you. This procedure will eliminate many extra calories spent sampling and eating until you find what you want.

If you go to a restaurant, don't eat the entire meal to get to the cheesecake, if what you really wanted was the cheesecake. It is OK to order a side dish rather than an entire dinner. Don't be afraid to take home part of your meal in a doggie bag or to share a large portion with a friend.

Belinda learned to listen to her inner knowledge the hard way. One night she had a strong desire to eat shrimp. She went to a local restaurant for dinner. When she entered, she saw that the special for the day was a hamburger plate with all the fixings for just $3.95, while a shrimp dinner cost $7.95. The common sense part of Belinda couldn't pass up a bargain, so she ordered the hamburger special and ate it all. Afterward she was full but unsatisfied and wanted to binge. She learned that she had discounted her real desires to save money.

If you learn to listen to your inner self, you can eat what you want and feel satisfied and powerful. What you desire will not always be junk food or high-calorie food. Sometimes you will crave a piece of chicken or a bowl of soup. When you are true to yourself, you will find that food is a friend, not an enemy.

Changing your behavior while you are with people in a social situation involving food is a challenge to handling your life and your food effectively. Social settings present two possible dangers: the temptation of foods you usually don't allow yourself to eat and the pressure to act as others expect you to.

If you are beginning to consider not dieting anymore and learning to make educated choices, you will be desensitizing yourself about certain formerly fearful foods like cake and bread. In addition, you will soon learn to go to a party or buffet and consciously choose only certain foods without feeling deprived.

A good technique to use for brunches, buffets, or potlucks is to take a tour of the food table without a plate in your hand. Look at and evaluate everything. You know what potato salad tastes like. How many times have you tasted it in your life? Hundreds of times, probably. Look over the array and choose the three foods you simply cannot pass up without feeling deprived. Make sure you have a moderate portion of each one. Keep reminding yourself that most of the other foods are those you have had all your life; they are ordinary and uninteresting.

Another way to handle the experience is to take a tablespoon of everything if you really want it all. By taking a taste, you will satisfy the fear of being deprived but will have limited your calories.

When faced with a social situation involving food or a holiday meal with traditional foods that you get only once a year, you will find that a simple approach is to problem solve before you are tempted. Do not wait until you are actually seated at the feast; take a few minutes the day before that holiday or wedding reception and think about the foods you will be encountering. Pick out the problem aspects of the event; will you be upset by the amount of food, the types of foods, or the idea that celebrations should be times for throwing caution to the winds and starting a diet afresh the next day? Ask yourself what you can do to change the situation into one that is both enjoyable and guilt-free.

HANDLING SOCIAL SITUATIONS

To deal with large gatherings and social times, you will have to understand the idea that each person has some experiences in her life that are *safe* and some that are *dangerous*. Each food abuser must become sensitive to the amount of danger in a given event and learn how to take care of herself.

Family feasts such as Christmas or Thanksgiving are terribly stressful for many bingers. Anorectics, bulimics, and overeaters are afraid that others are looking at their plates and judging them for what they are eating. Every time Leila attended a family get-together, she would eat and later vomit. Leila is a former anorectic who is still very thin. She is tempted by the foods at these dinners and upset by the fear of calling attention to herself or of worrying her family because they think she doesn't eat enough. To assuage their fear, she eats large amounts but later purges. In the long run, she is hurting herself more by doing this than by facing up to them.

I taught Leila to view the family dinners in terms of what feels safe and dangerous to her. A short time later, her aunt took her out to dinner. She knew that trying to eat what she thought others thought she should eat was a dangerous act. She ordered a salad while the others ordered complete dinners. In this instance, a salad was safe because she could enjoy it and not throw up. In choosing the salad, she did something powerful. She diagnosed her own need and took care of it. Eating a full meal might have pleased her aunt, but the cost was too dear. Soon Leila began to feel less anxious about family eating experiences. She was able to eat more foods, but only the foods and amounts that seemed safe each time.

Who has power over your eating behavior? Make a list of important people in your life. You may want to put someone on your list who is dead but still influences you. Next to each name write what this person wants or expects of you. Is it something you agree with or feel resentful or angry about? Why do you think they know better than you about how to run your life? Cross out all the "shoulds" that others have imposed on you that you do not want to be bound to. Now make a list of what you want for yourself that is reasonable and loving.

Remember, *what other people think about you is none of your business*! When you look into yourself and recognize that everyone who loves you wants you to feel good, you can give yourself permission to eat only what you can deal with without purging or feeling guilty.

Reading about how to change can be informative and exciting, but actually to do it is sometimes difficult. When you find yourself resisting change, you may begin to hate yourself and may quit without giving yourself enough time to find ways to overcome your resistance. Working with a therapist or support group can help you to push past the stumbling block and learn to confront your conflicts and fears. The important thing is to dedicate yourself to the idea that you can overcome food addiction——no matter what it takes.

One of the techniques I use with my clients to promote immediate changes is to share a meal with them. I call this "restaurant therapy." You don't need a therapist to do this yourself, but you will need another person you can trust. You may want to ask a close friend or your spouse to share a meal if he or she can remain objective. But whether you are an overeater who is fat or bulimic, or an anorectic who is afraid of food, this experience may prove exceptionally worthwhile.

Pick a restaurant that you can afford and make sure it has a large menu that offers many different choices. A pleasant coffee shop may fit the bill well. Make sure you can order side dishes and do not have to commit yourself to an expensive full-course lunch or dinner. Pick any meal of the day you want. You may choose either the easiest or the most troublesome.

Explain to your companion that you are performing an experiment in order to find out more about yourself. The other person needs to promise to be supportive and not make any judgmental comments such as "Is that all you want? But you only ate a bite and left all the rest." Or, "Are you sure you want all of that? Isn't that awfully fattening?"

Here is a list of questions that you can have your helper ask you as you progress through the meal. You may want to add your own questions.

RESTAURANT THERAPY

1. As you are seated, look around and take stock of the situation. Ask yourself how anxious or fearful you are on a scale of 1 to 10. Talk about the anxiety or fear. What are you telling yourself? If you are very anxious, explore alternative ideas to calm yourself.

2. Take the menu and look through it quickly. Rate your level of anxiety again, 1 to 10. What are your thoughts?

3. With your friend, discuss the menu in great detail. Which foods or areas of food (desserts, sandwiches, drinks) are you telling yourself are strictly out of bounds? Why? What are your rules about these foods? What are the labels you put on them? Many of my clients will not eat bread because they have labeled it fattening. (A slice of bread has approximately 75 calories.)

4. How hungry are you now? Are you eating because you should? How much food do you really want? How much food can you allow yourself to eat? Are the answers the same for both these questions or do you keep yourself hungry? What are you telling yourself about portions and amounts of food on this menu?

5. Which foods on the menu make you feel safe? Why? What are your beliefs about these foods?

6. Pretend that you are dining with someone else who may not be as sympathetic to your problem as your present companion. What do you imagine that person would expect of you? How much and what

kind of foods would you feel you had to order and/or eat to please that person or others? Be specific. Name at least three important people in your life with whom eating is uncomfortable for you. What do you think they might be thinking when you are together? What do they actually say to you at the table? How do you feel about each one? How would you like it to be?

7. Check your level of anxiety or fear again. Where is it now? Are you feeling any more comfortable?

8. Close the menu. Think about the taste or texture sensation that you would like to have right now. Do you want hot or cold food, a large or small amount, chewy, crunchy, or smooth; salty, sweet, sour, or spicy? Imagine what food or foods would fit the bill. Name the food. Is this a food you allow yourself to eat? How do you feel about eating it? How much do you want? Is it on the menu? If it is not, are you willing to ask the waitress if you can get it, such as one scrambled egg or half a chef's salad? (Don't forget that you and your friend can agree to share portions.)

9. What do you want to order? Do it now.

10. When the food comes, what do you tell yourself? Have you specified that you wanted tomato instead of potato? Have you requested dressing on the side or no bread? Is the food the way you want it to be? Rate your state of anxiety.

11. Please eat your meal or snack. Converse with your partner. Occasionally relate any thoughts or feelings that are either positive or negative. You may find yourself wanting to leave food and afraid of what

the other will think. Continue to talk about how the food tastes and how you feel about eating it in front of someone else.

12. If your friend and companion is a person who never worries about food or weight, encourage him/her to share his/her thoughts and feelings with you. Compare your ideas. What have you learned?

13. At the end of the meal, review the experience. How do you feel right now? Are there any social situations coming up in the near future that you can discuss and rethink right now with your friend? How is your anxiety level now?

Changing what you do is only the first level of transformation. As you have gone through the suggested activities in this chapter, you may find that you are already involved with both your emotions and your thoughts about yourself and food. It is impossible to alter what you do without affecting other aspects of yourself. Behavioral modification, however, is the easiest level to start with. Changing your eating behavior is a specific and concrete experience. You can take small steps that are significant. You can chart your food intake and work from the written data. You can pinpoint specific meals or binge-eating episodes. Dealing with feelings and thoughts that go on all day long is more complex, but you must learn how to do that, too, or you will not have positive, lasting results.

CHANGING HOW YOU FEEL

Most food abusers haven't a glimmer of feeling or a hint of what has triggered the binge at the moment they start. Perhaps later they realize what has upset them, or perhaps it is buried too quickly and too deep, but it is there below the surface. With some careful questioning, the feelings will come to light. This is what happened with Carol.

Carol came to see me after a two-week binge. She did not know what was upsetting her. I asked what had been happening lately and discovered that Carol's aged aunt had offered to take her on a trip to another state to visit relatives. Carol could not afford the trip herself and was delighted at the gift. But the aunt kept procrastinating and did not make arrangements. Finally, Carol found out that her aunt intended to make the trip possible only if she would lose weight. Carol was not consciously aware of her anger toward her aunt, but she was so upset that she had spent two weeks eating. Carol had turned her anger inward and was "eating at" the person she felt angry with. Many nonassertive people refuse to speak of their anger and go home and "pig-out" instead.

Behind most anger is *fear*. The angry person feels vulnerable and open to hurt, so she protects herself by masking the fear with feelings of anger and resentment. Carol felt guilty because she was angry at a helpless old woman. That was not nice, she thought. She was afraid that people would think she was a terrible person if she defied or confronted her aunt.

Carol is a typical example of a person who is unaware of her negative feelings. She does not allow herself either to know how she feels or to express the feelings. To stop binge eating, you need to accept the fact that you are hiding feelings from yourself and you are not dealing with your feelings in an appropriate way.

WHAT ARE FEELINGS?

A common problem for bingers is that they say "think" when they should say "feel" and say "feel" when they should say "think." "I *feel* that I need a support system" and "I *feel* that you aren't helping me" are two cases in point. If the speaker doesn't know the difference between a feeling and a thought, she will have trouble understanding the dynamics of her binge behavior. In each of the two sentences, the word *think* should be substituted for the word feel: "I *think* that I need a support system" and "I *think* that you aren't helping me." Feel refers to a feeling, a sensation or emotion, not a thought. What comes after the word *feel* should be the name of a feeling: "I feel upset when you yell at me" or "I feel frightened when I go to big parties." It may take practice, and when you learn to separate your feelings from your thoughts, you will be able to understand the four-level plan for change more clearly.

You can divide the range of human emotions into four basic classifications: mad, glad, sad, and scared. Here is a list of variations that you may want to use:

MAD: resentful, irritated, furious, annoyed, offended, irate, frustrated, fuming, boiling, indignant, cross, bitter, enraged, hateful, disinterested

GLAD: happy, satisfied, serene, comfortable, joyous, pleased, ecstatic, excited, exhilarated, thrilled, relaxed, enthusiastic, cheery, lighthearted, proud, warm

SAD: unhappy, depressed, gloomy, ashamed, discouraged, heavyhearted, disappointed, in the dumps, blah, dismal, melancholy, sullen, discontented, embarrassed, useless

SCARED: afraid, timid, panicky, alarmed, insecure, nervous, anxious, worried, dismayed, threatened, petrified, shaky, terrified, cautious, frightened, mixed-up, uptight, abandoned

These are only a few samples of the many words that can help you to become more sensitive to what is happening inside you.

I caution you to beware of what I call "umbrella words." An umbrella word is a common word that is too general in meaning. "Nervous," "good," and "bad" are three umbrella words. Fay would tell me each week that she ate because she felt nervous. When I asked Fay to explain "nervous," we discovered that sometimes it meant angry and other times it meant sad or frustrated. Fay used "nervous" to explain any intense feeling. Once she eliminated the word *nervous* from her vocabulary and replaced it with more precise words to describe her emotions, she could see that each binge was triggered by a different feeling associated with a separate experience or situation. She then started to deal with stress-producing occasions successfully.

Here is a simple exercise to practice naming your feelings. Take a piece of paper and complete the following sentence twenty times. You may want to address each one to a different person in your life or all of them to just one person. Do ten sets in which you use positive feelings and ten that express negative emotions.

I feel _____,
when you do/say _____.

EMOTIONS AND HUNGER

There are individuals who learn in early childhood to confuse hunger with emotional anxiety or physical discomfort. When a baby cries, the parent usually thinks it is hungry and will attempt to feed the child. A baby may cry for a number of reasons: he may have a cramp, be startled, or wet. Since the baby can't talk, the parent has to guess. Many children are continually given food as a message that "this will make you feel good." I have seen parents at playgrounds who pick up a crying toddler who has just taken a spill and say, "Don't cry, sweetheart, have a cookie. You're all right." If the child gets used to receiving food in response to negative experiences, she will associate food with the solution. Even as an adult, this person may continue to use food to soothe unhappy feelings.

When a toddler falls down in the playground and screams in pain or fear, and you offer the child a candy or cookie, you actually are rejecting the child's feelings. You are saying, "There is nothing really wrong. Here is something nice to distract you." The child may not be hurt but may feel scared or surprised, maybe a bit scuffed. By giving food and distraction, you teach the child to deny her own feelings. Then when she grows up, she will continue to "eat down" and discount unhappy feelings automatically. It would be much better for the parent to pick up the child, give her a hug, and say, "I can see that you are upset. Let's take a look at your knee, wash it off, and see if you need a Band-Aid." If you acknowledge the child's feelings, you are teaching her to affirm herself.

How many of you give yourself a special food when you aren't feeling well? I call these "Mommy foods" because they are usually what Mommy gave you when you were sick. Examples of such foods are oatmeal or farina mixed with milk, rice, baked potato, tea and toast, 7-Up, soda crackers, chicken soup, or Jell-O. Do you see that you are creating a certain mood when you eat these foods? It is as if someone loving were watching over you, pampering you again.

One way you can begin to teach yourself to differentiate between hunger, anxiety, and physical discomfort is to ask yourself two questions when you are reaching for food and you know you are not truly hungry. The first question is: "What is going on?" Ask this question a few times, and you will be amazed at the answers that are readily available to you. What is bothering you may have happened twenty-four or forty-eight hours ago, even a week ago, and you have suppressed the anger, resentment, fear, or guilt. Finally, the emotional energy gets too great and bursts out. To quiet yourself, you find yourself reaching for something to eat. What is going on? Some possible answers might be: My husband forgot our anniversary; the mechanic said the car was fixed, but I can't start it, and I have a meeting to attend; my mother is sick; I don't know how to pay my bills this month; I'm lonely.

The second question concerns how to know what you are feeling, when it is not hunger. See if you can name the feeling that goes with your upset: angry, sad, bored, demeaned, left out, surprised, frightened, helpless, overjoyed. When you learn to tell the difference between these feelings and emotional hunger, you are on your way to success.

ANGER

Anger is a build-up of energy that results from feeling threatened. Frustration is usually felt when someone or something is threatening your well-being in some way and you think you can't or shouldn't take action to combat the situation. The feelings of anger and frustration lead to a change in your body: increased heartbeat, output of adrenalin, and so on. Your body mobilizes for action, but nothing happens. It is as if you assembled troops for a skirmish and called it off without telling the troops where to go or what to do. The anger energy then seeks another outlet or target: the body, the "self," or some other "safe" object.

When you were growing up, did you learn that anger was bad? Did you learn that *you* were bad if you were angry? Were you told to "stop it"? How can you turn off anger? Where do you put it? Did you learn to push it down and put on a happy face? What happened to the anger? It remained, smoldering, never quite put out.

Anger is a feeling just as joy is a feeling. To deny it is to set yourself up for problems. Although it is perfectly healthy to feel angry, it is *not* OK to hurt others or destroy property in your rage. *You are entitled to your feelings, but you are also responsible for your behavior.* Holding on to old anger and pretending it does not exist can make you a very unhappy person.

There are a number of ways you can deal with current anger. When you are feeling red-hot rage, you can pound a pillow in your bedroom or some other private place. Hit your bed or sofa cushion with a tennis racket or golf club or baseball bat, pretending that the cushion is the person you are angry with. Shout any words that come to mind. If you have no tennis racket, use a rolled-up newspaper or wet towel and hit a table or sink counter. Another satisfying technique is to throw ice cubes outside against a hard wall. They shatter like glass but leave nothing to clean up. Be sure to yell when you throw them!

If all else fails, try screaming. You can scream in the shower, if you don't want your neighbors to wonder. The best place for screaming may be in your car with all the windows rolled up. Any of these activities will release much tension and anger energy. *Then you can decide how to proceed to resolve the problem.*

Feeling anger does not necessarily mean that you hurl venom at another person. Often the situation begins and ends with you, but you must allow yourself to take a look at it. After you have yelled and pounded, write an angry letter but don't mail it! Wait an hour and reread the letter. Ask yourself what you have learned from the letter. Many people discover that the other person really did not do anything, but you, the angry one, reacted from a personal bias. Do you feel that your anger is finished? What do you need to do to end this problem?

Do you hold on to anger? What do you get out of it? Some people hold grudges for years, often forgetting the cause of the resentment, but fanning the flames of anger like glowing coals. You can choose to release old anger simply by tearing up the letter and announcing to yourself that the past is past.

Edna was an anger collector. She was still actively upset over happenings of thirty years ago. Edna lovingly brought out her memories of how people hurt her, discounted her, or slighted her over the years and recounted them excitedly as if she were sharing her photo album of adventures and trips.

Each time someone hurt her or let her down, it was an excuse to slink home and lick her wounds by comforting herself with food. When I asked Edna how her anger was her friend, she replied, "It keeps me warm." Anger and resentment act like a shot of adrenalin for Edna. When she feels the strong waves of rage, she feels alive.

Here is how I helped Edna get rid of her old angers. I asked her to take a number of 3 x 5 cards and to write on each card the title of her angry memory and one sentence about it. I had her read each one out loud and ask herself if she had truly had enough of that incident and was ready to be finished with it. One by one, she perused the cards and burned each one that she was ready to release. She made a good fire in the fireplace. Although the memories remain, Edna no longer feels the anger or resentment. Today, instead of looking for the worst in people to confirm her fantasies and give her an excuse to eat, she looks for the best in her new friends. She also tells people when they have said or done something she doesn't like. She doesn't collect anger, she dispels it. Today Edna is smiling more and eating less.

It is simple to clean out the skeletons in your closet of bad feelings. Write an "Angry Book." Get a notebook. Make a list of all the people and events from your past and your present that you still feel anger or resentment about. You will be surprised that you may still feel angry toward the kids in your third-grade class who made fun of you during recess. Write down all your unfinished business. Finish it now, even if some of the people on your list are no longer alive.

Start anywhere on your list. Pick a topic that appeals to you at the moment and begin to write. Spelling and grammar are not important because no one but you will see these pages. Put your book in a safe place to protect your personal thoughts. Use whatever language best expresses your feelings. Keep writing until you have run out of topics and exhausted your grudge list. Then read the book and think about it. How do you feel? What do you want to do? When you feel finished, burn your writing or destroy it. When you have let go of all that garbage, you will feel a wonderful sense of release. If any old angers return to haunt you, remind yourself that you have buried them and that they no longer can bother you.

Getting rid of old angers doesn't mean that you will no longer feel any angry feelings. Events will occur in your life that you don't like. Keep current. Know your feelings, express them, and resolve them. Don't let angry sludge clog up your emotional system.

FEAR

Anger and fear are usually related. Priscilla was a compulsive overeater who had gained thirty-five pounds. She was eating because she was enraged with her husband. But she was also afraid of expressing her anger. She was angry because her husband had lost interest in sex and rarely made love to her. He refused to see a doctor, minister, therapist, or anyone else for consultation about the problem. Priscilla was angry because they sat home, watched TV, and had a very dull time. She was forty years old. Priscilla wanted more out of life, even though her husband was a good provider and a fine father. She had many good years ahead and did not want to spend the rest of her life this way. She was unwilling to force the issue with her husband, however, because she was afraid. She was terrified of being single again. She thought she might be too old to find a new mate, and she was too fat! She surmised that if she lost weight and looked appealing, she definitely would not stand for her husband's problem remaining unsolved. If she were thinner, she would have to take action. It was too frightening to contemplate.

Staying angry at her husband gave her an excuse to overeat and stay fat and never find out that her life could be happier.

If you are a binge eater, think of someone in your life whom you "eat at." What is your anger about? What are you really afraid of? What is the worst thing that might happen if you confront your anger and take a stand? Is it worth it? *What do you deserve?*

Fear stops many food abusers from expressing anger or asking for what they want. They fear the consequences of being open with feelings . . . fear loss of approval or fear loss of love.

One of the common misconceptions about feelings is the belief that if you say "no," you may hurt someone else's feelings. You cannot hurt a person by exerting your rights to your own life. For others to base their happiness on your behavior is emotional blackmail. To believe that you are responsible for making someone happy is to offer yourself into a life of bondage to the whims of another. "If you loved me, you would . . ." is a poisonous statement.

People-pleasing keeps the "good girl" in a position of powerlessness in respect to the person given the power to bestow approval or love. People with low self-esteem, like food addicts, often look to others for a sense of worth. They consider almost everyone else better, smarter, happier, or more worthy.

Let's take a closer look at fears. Here is a list of fears that you may identify with. Take each one and, on a scale of 1 to 10, indicate how strong the fear is in your life today:

abandonment, change, looking foolish, rejection, pain, isolation, loss of love, sickness, financial problems, success, failure, death.

You may find that it is helpful to draw a picture of your fear or fears. You may draw one picture that encompasses all your fears or a separate picture for each one. Draw different colors or shapes rather than specific objects. Think about how you feel when you are afraid and where in your body you feel the fear. See if you can put that feeling into your picture.

Now write about each fear that you think is hampering you today. Ask yourself what you are getting out of holding on to your fear. (Do you get attention from others? Do you get to control others?) Think about how your life would be without this fear. How ready are you to let go of it? Be sure to write your conclusion: "I have decided to . . ."

Fear of success and fear of failure are often underlying reasons for hanging on to compulsive eating habits. It may seem incredible that a food addict is actually reluctant to be free of a debilitating problem. It will make sense if you realize that the symptom—the binge or purge—is merely a distraction from the primary problem.

People who are afraid of failing will keep themselves afloat with worries about overcoming an eating disorder. Eating and trying to stop eating takes up a great amount of time and keeps them from facing reality. It enables them to sit on the sidelines and fantasize about what they wish they could have but don't think they could ever achieve because they feel inadequate. Those with low self-esteem cannot afford to compete for jobs, friendships, or love relationships because they don't think they can be successful and are too afraid of the pain of finding out that their worst fears are correct.

Fear of failure means giving the right to judge you as adequate over to the others whom you deem better or more worthy. Take a piece of paper and write the word *they* on top. Now make a list of who *they* are. Who are the people you are worried about pleasing or displeasing? Next to each name list the things that person expects from you. What is the worst that will happen if you don't meet those expectations? Differentiate between the things on your list that you think you should do but really don't like or want and those that you would really feel happy accomplishing. Cross out all the "should" things you feel coerced into doing. Make a new list of just those things you choose for yourself.

Fear of failure is increased when you are constantly comparing yourself to others. Do you judge your insides by other people's outsides?

The next time you enter a room full of people, give yourself this task. Instead of dwelling on how different you are from each one, look for all the ways you are similar to others. Begin with very simple things such as, we all have two eyes, sleep in beds, know how to write our names, watch television, get wet when it rains, and want to be loved. Keep doing this wherever you go; notice how your anxiety begins to disappear.

Fear of success can also be a factor in eating disorders. If you believe that those who succeed are so rare and so special that they are left all alone at the pinnacle, success may seem to be only for those who are willing to be alone and friendless. "People won't like me because I'm too good" is an excuse for staying mediocre or failing. Fear of rejection or isolation are two ingredients of fear of success. Worries about succeeding and finding that once you've "made it" there's nothing left in life is another fantasy.

A majority of food abusers seem to feel unworthy or bad when they are not productive. They are constantly striving but don't know where they are going or whether they should allow themselves to achieve their goals, so they detour into compulsive eating as a delaying tactic.

One way of getting ready for success is to allow others to notice you and praise you. Here is an experiment that is easy to do and feels good. Look at yourself in the mirror and choose something about yourself that you like—your eyes, smile, skin, nails, sense of humor, or warmth. Every morning and evening when you are washing, tell yourself out loud ten times, "I like my _____." Within a week you will notice that other people begin to tell you that you have a lovely smile or a terrific sense of humor, or whatever you have concentrated on. When you allow yourself to be OK in some way, you are also giving permission to others to see you that way. (More than 75 percent of human communication is nonverbal, so you don't always have to say how you feel; you will just naturally show it.)

Keep giving yourself compliments on your looks and your abilities. Refrain from turning away compliments. If someone else likes something about you, and you don't agree, just grit your teeth and say, "Thank you." Then take the compliment home and consider that maybe it is the truth. At first, receiving praise may feel painful, but with practice it becomes more and more pleasurable.

Another way to get ready for success is to study those people you admire the most. Look for the traits and powers that they have. Realize that they are also human and have flaws, yet they are able to achieve goals and be successful. Make a list of your positive traits and skills. If you can't think of more than one or two, call your best friend and ask for help. Make a list of at least twenty positive things about yourself. Post it and read it to yourself every day. This is not pride or self-centeredness; it is the truth. You are entitled to know the truth about yourself!

NEGATIVE EMOTIONS

Almost everyone suffering from an eating disorder feels depressed. If you are seriously depressed and find that you are not sleeping well and are having trouble functioning in your daily life, sometimes feeling too low even to get out of bed, see your doctor for diagnosis and treatment. Some depressions are the result of chemical imbalance. Many bingers are depressed to a lesser extent. They experience a sense of weariness and a deadening of feelings.

Depression and anger are often interrelated. Under the depressed feelings, you may find unexpressed anger. Sometimes the anger is so strong that you shut down all systems to contain the rage, so that you are aware only of your lethargy. Most depressed addictive eaters feel like victims. They see their situation as impossible and unchangeable. Feelings of helplessness and hopelessness result. You may want to seek therapy to deal with depression.

Boredom is the second cousin of depression. A common excuse for binging is boredom: "I had nothing to do so I ate." Boredom is not a primary feeling, but it is a way of covering over other feelings, even in the midst of many opportunities for excitement. Refer to the list of feelings earlier in this chapter and find the ones that may be beneath the surface of your boredom. You may want to start by asking yourself if you are suppressing anxiety, resentment, fear, guilt, or sadness.

Strong feelings of guilt contribute to many binges. If the food abuser is not feeling guilty before the binge, she usually feels guilty after the binge. Bulimics feel additional guilt because of their shame about purging.

Guilt is a waste of time! Guilt comes from not living up to expectations, the *shoulds* or *should nots*. One of my favorite sayings is: *What other people say about me is none of my business!* If you are willing to be responsible for the outcome of your decisions and your behavior, you no longer need to feel guilt.

Some people are so addicted to guilt that they continually seek out situations that make them feel guilty. Connie called me to say that she would no longer be counseling with me because I was too nice! She preferred to go to Weight Watchers again so she could be weighed in and given a specific eating plan. That way, if she were bad, she would know it. She needed to be given rules and regulations to follow. Knowing whether she was "good" or "bad" was comforting to her. I do not use those words. I help people explore their behavior to help them learn more about their own choices. Some people feel very frightened when no policemen are around to guide them.

POSITIVE FEELINGS

Positive feelings also can be a cue for a binge. A person with low self-esteem may believe that she is not entitled to as much happiness as someone else she is comparing herself to. Happiness may feel threatening to this person. She might binge to feel so bad that she then has an excuse for not attending a party or receiving love. One bulimic woman, after an intense binge/purge night, called her boy friend to break up with him because she thought she didn't deserve such a wonderful relationship.

Spoiling a special moment by abusing food or hanging on to self-hatred is a way of avoiding happiness. Such people feel that too much of a good thing is forbidden; therefore, they must either cut off the joyous feeling or keep themselves from experiencing it at all.

Another irrational belief about dealing with happiness is to let yourself have it as long as you have paid for it. Some bingers don't want to enter into such a bargain because they believe that the price will be pain, so they are content not to reach the heights of joy. Others keep score to make sure that they have had enough hard luck or self-induced punishment to merit the few moments of happiness they allow themselves. I recall a client saying, "When I feel pain at least I know I'm alive."

SELF-DISCOUNT: DENYING FEELINGS

Once you are acquainted with the nature of your feelings—mad, glad, sad, or scared—and are willing to acknowledge that you do have these emotions, the second

189

step in the process is to stop lying to yourself about how deeply these feelings really do upset you. I call this "self-discount." A discount is a way of devaluing something, marking it down in worth, denying it. Addictive people often devalue themselves before anyone else can.

When you discount your own feelings, you are burying them alive. They will come back to haunt you in the form of a binge. Maxine binged all weekend but didn't know why. Saturday had been her wedding anniversary, but it was also her father's birthday. She had insisted on staying home all day Saturday to cook a large meal as a double celebration. That set her off, and she continued to overeat nonstop for the next two days. When I asked Maxine what she would have done if she could have had her choice, she instantly replied that she wanted to spend a romantic evening alone with her husband to celebrate. But, she quickly went on to explain, it wasn't nice to leave out her father since it was also his birthday. Maxine felt guilty if she wasn't putting herself last all the time. Since she ignored most of her own needs and desires, she was usually filled with frustration and anger, which she suppressed because that, too, wasn't nice. Consequently, she was a constant compulsive eater.

One phrase that self-discounters use is "That's silly." Gerry binged because her family forgot her birthday. She secretly wanted them to fuss over her without being reminded. They didn't. She told herself that since she was a grown-up she shouldn't mind. "Birthdays are for kids." There is within each person a fun-loving part or child self. Some individuals think that because they look like adults, they must put away that aspect of themselves that can be silly, laugh, giggle, and play. Thus they become 100 percent parent. When you tell yourself that something is silly, or for kids, your parent-self is trying to deny you the opportunity to have pleasure as a free spirit. Wanting to have a birthday party or a costume party, hang up your stocking at Christmas, or have an Easter basket is your right.

One way of learning whether you discount yourself is to make a list of all things you think are silly or childish that you don't allow yourself to do. Read the list over and think about those things that you don't do but would really like to do. Give yourself permission to do them!

You may also have learned to hide your feelings from others and from yourself because you thought it might be impolite to reveal them. The phrase, "It doesn't matter," reflects a self put-down. You can test yourself to find the difference between not expressing your thoughts and feelings out of politeness or of fear of rejection or disapproval this way: After an incident when you were "polite," did you later have a stomachache, tension, or a binge? If you have a delayed reaction to a situation in which you held your tongue or "played along," it means that you were denying your true feelings and the right to express them.

One excuse for denying feelings is that you think you can't do anything about the situation. Alba's eating was totally out of control. Her husband had been laid off and things were very hard for them, but Alba refused to admit how anxious and afraid she was. She denied her feelings and ate instead. Once she faced her fear and learned ways to reduce the stress, her binges diminished.

Until you can admit your feelings to yourself or another, change cannot occur. Remember that when you tell yourself, "It shouldn't bother me," you mean that something is bothering you and you don't want to acknowledge it. The hardest part of changing the power your feelings have over you is to admit that some things are upsetting you. Once you take your emotional temperature and find that it is high, you can do something to bring the emotional fever down. If you pretend that things are fine when they aren't, you will continue to have chronic binges.

The second level of the four-level plan for permanent change teaches the food abuser to recognize the emotion and the degree of intensity and correlate them to a specific event or relationship in her life. But feelings aren't facts! Even if the anger, guilt, fear, or anxiety are overwhelming, the key to the binge lies somewhere else—in level three— changing how you think.

CHANGING HOW YOU THINK

Moods change as feelings change. Most people have had the experience of suddenly having an emergency arise at a time when they are feeling blue or slightly ill. They rise to the occasion and handle the emergency, leaving the depression or illness at home.

What starts a feeling and what stops it? Your thoughts and ideas. Your feelings are your reactions to your existing thoughts and ideas concerning what's safe or threatening, good or bad, attractive or repulsive.

Melanie was very upset when she came for her therapy session. She felt angry with her boy friend. I asked her how long she intended to hold on to her angry feelings. She was amazed at my question and thought I was a little weird for suggesting that she could define a time limit for her anger. I insisted that she decide whether it would be a two-hour mad, a twelve-hour rage, or a three-day tantrum. She decided that she would be angry until dinner time that night. I asked her to report back to me whether she had let go of her anger at the designated time. She did.

Feelings and behaviors result from thoughts and beliefs that you are not often conscious of. Melanie thought that feelings were like rainstorms that came at nature's bidding, were sometimes light and sometimes intense, and ended in their own time and in their own way. She learned that she was responsible for her anger. She had turned it on in reaction to something that had occurred; she also could learn to turn it off at will.

You feel happy or miserable because of your ideas about what is happening. When a car mechanic reports that you need $200 worth of work done on your car, you can either feel happy or unhappy. If you tell yourself that you are always having car trouble, that you never have enough money, that bad things always happen to you, you will depress yourself. If you tell yourself that you are lucky the mechanic found the problem and saved you from a terrible accident, that now you can feel safe driving, that you are glad you take good care of your car, you will feel happy about paying for the repair.

Each of you has a running conversation going on in your head day and night. This inner dialogue is very private and rarely shared with others. What you tell yourself in the privacy of your head drastically influences how you feel and what you do. To change your behavior with food, you must change your ideas and the commands you give yourself.

WHAT ARE YOU TELLING YOURSELF?

Since this voice is your special inner friend or inner controller, you may not realize that much of what you tell yourself is not the truth. It is only an opinion that you accept as the gospel. To find out how much is true and how much is irrational belief, write down some of these thoughts or share them with someone you can trust—someone who will help you reevaluate your ideas and rewrite the faulty ones.

An easy way to start is to look at a recent situation that triggered a binge. Name the feeling that you were reacting to or trying to suppress. Then complete this sentence:

I feel _____ because I am telling myself

_____ .

Tim, an actor who did not get a part, wrote: "I feel rejected and scared because I am telling myself that I will always be alone. No one will want me and I will be alone and die." Tim has had many rejections but hasn't died. He has lived through each one. We analyzed the process of Tim's experience with rejection and found out that he goes through three stages when he doesn't get hired:

1. Pain
2. Realization that there will be other opportunities and other parts
3. Healing

In spite of knowing this, he tells himself that he will die, and he scares himself so much that he escapes into a binge. Tim has learned that he can now rewrite the message in his head. He can assure himself that when he loses out on a role, he will go through a three-stage healing process, and he will live through it and be able to pursue his career with less anxiety.

Yvonne's statement was, "I feel depressed and tearful about my job because I tell myself that they lied to me when I was hired, my boss shows favoritism to another woman, and they never give me what I want." Yvonne binges constantly because she keeps reviewing four gripes in a dirge about her job:

- She was hired as a secretary with a promise that there would be a chance to advance. After three years she has not been given more responsibility or opportunity.
- The boss is dating a woman in the office, and Yvonne feels left out of their twosome.
- Yvonne does better work than the other woman, who gets away with incompetence.
- Yvonne would like approval from her boss but is often discounted by him.

Each time Yvonne goes through her litany of unhappiness, she reinforces her feelings of frustration and anger.

By taking the energy she had invested in feeling anger and helplessness and reinvesting it in reasoning and problem solving, Yvonne was able to rewrite her dirge as follows:

- I am just a secretary but I have fun at my job and get to meet many fascinating people. I may still have a chance to get something better. If that doesn't happen here, in the near future, I will look for a new job.

- My boss and his girl friend are a twosome. I can get my own boyfriend.
- Some people in this world do get away with incompetent work. I can either accept it or change jobs.
- My boss is not interested in my feelings. He is not always polite when he is worried about business.

Yvonne changed her thoughts about her job, and she felt much happier. There are many exciting aspects of her work that she was downplaying by focusing only on what she wasn't getting.

GARDEN PATCH PHILOSOPHY

If you look at the world as if it were a garden, you will find that all the people in it are like flowers and plants. Some people are roses or violets; others are like shrubs or wild flowers. Some are weeds; some are vegetables. Yvonne was expecting her boss to be a rose. In fact, he is a cabbage. She keeps feeling disappointed and angry when he doesn't act like a rose. She forgets to admire the cabbageness of him. Instead of feeling upset when he rushes out of the office at closing time without waiting for her, Yvonne can stop hoping he will miraculously change. Instead, she can feel relief when he rushes past her, telling herself, "That's just like him, rushing out without caring, but that's how cabbages are!"

III: A Self-Help Program for Change

By using the garden patch philosophy, you can stop being upset or frustrated when those nearest or dearest to you don't change even when you expect them to. Mildred felt constant disapproval from her eighty-year-old mother. No matter what she did, or said, her mother criticized or embarrassed her. I asked Mildred to make up a checklist of her mother's most irritating habits that she reacted to over and over again. Instead of cringing and waiting for the ax to fall and for the feelings of inadequacy and hurt to fill her, I taught Mildred to wait expectantly for the well-worn barbs about Mildred's looks, her weight, her clothes, and so on. Rather than reacting with angry feelings, I urged Mildred to choose a way to feel happy feelings. Mildred was to check off each complaint and each criticism to make sure her mother was running true to form. Instead of believing her mother's remarks, I suggested that Mildred chant in her inner voice, "That is just your opinion. It is not the truth about me." Once Mildred took away the power she had given her mother all these years, she was able to spend time with her without reacting negatively and binging.

When you accept things as they are and stop expecting people to change, you will not be as helpless as you may think. Instead, you will have the power to decide what *you* want to do about the relationship. You have the choice of accepting the other people and situations by changing your attitude, or you can change the situations by removing yourself from them.

When you become aware that the *thought* precedes the *feeling*, moreover, you will be able to stop *reacting* to life and start to *respond*. A reaction is like the knee-jerk you get when the doctor taps your leg—you immediately let your feelings take over in a given situation. You may say things you later regret, or you may stifle what you wish to say or do.

A response is based on your having power to decide how you feel, what you think, and how you want to resolve the problem. The difference between a reaction and a response depends on who has the power. Mildred felt hurt by her mother's comments because Mildred thought her mother had the power to judge her as "good" or "acceptable." When Mildred affirmed that her mother's ideas were only opinions and not truth, Mildred took back the power and no longer had to believe the untruths. She could choose to tell herself good things despite her mother's criticism.

Expectations about how other people should act can also get you into trouble. If you think that others should be as considerate, sensitive, loyal, and reasonable as you are, you are expecting the world to be your clone. It may not seem fair, but each person is unique. Some are more loving, some more capable, some more honest than others.

Lee felt angry and frightened when his roommate had a loud temper tantrum. Lee was disillusioned. John had appeared to be a mellow and low-key guy, yet he created loud and angry scenes. Lee would never do that because he is extremely considerate of others. Lee discovered, however, that he was not as considerate as he thought. He was afraid of loud outbursts of feelings because his father had acted like that. As a child, Lee had become afraid of his father's temper. As an adult, he projects that fear on anyone who yells. His rationalization, however, is that other people should feel uncomfortable around someone who yells or slams doors. Because Lee is so sensitive to anger and afraid of those who express it freely, he assumed that everyone thinks poorly of angry people. He thought his roomate should automatically know that his expressions of anger were impolite and should feel ashamed of himself. In other words, Lee told himself that his roommate, John, should think and feel the same way Lee did.

My work with Lee involved helping him to realize that John wasn't his father. Lee recognized that John was a person who felt comfortable with occasional angry outbursts that didn't hurt anyone but just let off steam. Lee never showed anger but had frequent binges. When he acknowledged that John was a good roommate who sometimes expressed anger, Lee felt less afraid. He started to practice new ways to be aware of his own anger before he reached for food and learned to verbalize his negative feelings instead of eat them down.

YOUR PERSONAL BILL OF RIGHTS

A universal problem for all people with eating disorders is low self-esteem. To change your behavior, change your thoughts and feelings about yourself. You will achieve this when you begin to believe that you are adequate, good, lovable, and capable. Non-assertive people let others have their way without putting up a fight. The average binge eater says "yes" when she is thinking "no." She gives away her rights and doesn't stand up for her wants and beliefs, but rather does whatever is necessary to avoid making waves. One way to change your thoughts about yourself is to find out what rights you allow yourself to have.

Here is a list of personal rights that you may be afraid to act upon. Take each one and write your thoughts and your excuses for disallowing it. You will discover how you hold yourself back and create your own frustration at feeling powerless.

• *I have permission to put myself first.*

When you read these words, you may feel very uncomfortable. You may think that putting yourself first is selfish and an ego trip. Perhaps others have picked up on your belief in your inadequacy and taken advantage of you. When you think you are responsible for someone else's happiness, you are doomed to be treated like a servant. When will it be your turn for happiness or fun?

For twenty years, Sam had his aged mother come to his house every Sunday. He worked hard during the week and had only the weekend to spend with his wife and children. After all these years, he was angry about giving up his weekends. He told himself that a good son takes care of his mother. Sam wouldn't expect his children to feel so obligated toward him. When he began to put himself first, he found out that his mother could find other activities to keep herself occupied on Sunday.

• *I have permission to be the judge of my own feelings and to accept them as legitimate.*

I have already talked about self-discount. When you keep believing that others know you better than you know yourself, you are constantly suppressing feelings or judging yourself as "bad."

Judging your own feelings as "bad" or "silly" will not enable you to change them. Olivia was ashamed to admit that she had eaten all the candy out of her daughter's Christmas stocking. Olivia remembered how much fun it had been to have a stocking when she was a child. "Grown-ups don't have that kind of fun," Olivia believed. When she allowed herself to let the child part of her celebrate with a stocking of her own, she did not have to think of herself as less of an adult. Most adults have playthings and toys of some kind. Stuffed animals are no longer just for kids. Special mink teddy bears are being advertised for adults. Many grown women have hobbies of dollhouses and miniatures. Why not an Easter basket, a kite, or a doll?

- *I have permission to make mistakes.*
- *I have permission to change my mind or decide on a different course of action.*

I have put these two together because a person who does not allow herself to make mistakes cannot change her mind either. the problem for perfectionists is that they tell themselves that there is only one right way—and they don't know what it is. Anything they do may be wrong. They also believe that "Once I make my bed, I must lie in it." In other words, once you choose a path, you cannot deviate even if it proves uncomfortable or incorrect.

I usually ask people who are afraid of making mistakes to tell me the name of a perfect person. I have yet to find anyone who never errs. If nobody is perfect, why do you have to be? Entertain the notion that most people learn best from their mistakes. I have said throughout this book that the awful binge may be one of the best teachers you can have. Understanding binge eating can help you to change your life and experience more happiness than you ever dreamed possible.

It is also permissible to ignore the advice of others in your life. People-pleasers have trouble listening to their own hearts because they are usually thinking that someone else knows more, is luckier, or is more deserving. The more you like yourself and know that you have an inner knower or creative unconscious as an ally, the more you can risk going your own way. When you disagree with someone else's opinion or advice, ask yourself what is the worst thing that could happen if you followed your own intuition. Are you willing to accept the consequence of that action? If you are willing to take responsibility for your choice, go ahead and do what you really want.

- *I have permission to be alone, even when others want my company.*
- *I have permission to say "no."*

A person who is overly compliant usually feels anger and resentment toward those she goes along with. No one can read your mind to know what you really want. If you need time to yourself, not even your closest friend will know unless you say so.

Binge eaters often go along with others into situations where the food temptations are especially risky. I remember a young bulimic who was extremely tense because her parents were taking her out for her birthday to a buffet brunch. She was upset because she knew from past experience that buffets triggered feelings of being out of control. She told me that she intended to stuff herself and throw up. I pointed out that it was *her* birthday they were celebrating. I asked what her rights were as the person being honored. Until that moment, she hadn't realized that she could designate how she wanted to celebrate her birthday. She decided to request that they go to a restaurant with a regular menu. She didn't want to be surrounded by food but instead to be able to order one portion of what she liked. She knew that she could enjoy the meal and not vomit.

- *I have permission to not take responsibility for someone else's problem or happiness.*

Anorectics, bulimics, and compulsive overeaters maintain secrecy about their binges out of fear. They fear the judgment of others, and they fear that they will hurt a loved one. If a parent or spouse finds out about the binges, he or she may become upset. This attitude assumes that the food abuser thinks that she is responsible for someone else's good feelings.

I have lost count of all eating disorder patients I have counseled who are unpaid "psychotherapists." These individuals let others come to them with problems. The addictive eater tries to solve the problems and be a good friend or wise adviser but often takes the pain onto her own shoulders and eventually eats over it. She thinks there is no one for her to turn to. Some of my clients have told me, "I am the only one they level with and confide in." This leads to another problem shared by many food abusers.

- *I have permission to ask for help or support.*

One of the reasons that the public has only recently become aware of the problems of bulimia is that it is a very secret behavior. Bulimics tell themselves that they are disgusting and terrible people who should be ashamed of what they do. Because they worry that others will isolate or punish them by withdrawing love or approval, bulimics (and anorectics and compulsive overeaters) tell themselves that they should be able to handle the problem alone.

The more they try alone to overcome the compulsion for eating food, the greater the frustration when they fail. Sooner or later they give up and tell themselves that it is a hopeless task.

When someone tells me that she should be able to overcome binging by herself, I remind her that she doesn't fill her teeth herself or fix her car herself. Most of us have permission to ask for help when the problem is mechanical repair or ill health; eating disorders are like migraine headaches or persistent stomachaches. Compulsion to overeat is a real problem that most people cannot solve unaided. Recovery hinges on getting yourself that aid.

I have had clients who are afraid that I won't like them after I have learned the nature of their behavior. Part of my work is to reassure each one that what she eats is not a judgment of who she is but a signal of dis-ease in her life. Health professionals and fellow support-group members may be seen as allies in the battle. With support, you can win the fight.

It seems that the people who do overcome the eating syndromes are those who share their problem with someone who is willing to hear and to help. Talking to a friend may be the first step on the road to recovery. Not only are more health professionals, doctors, nutritionists, and psychotherapists specializing in eating disorders, but many self-help and support groups are forming all over the country.

Look at the eight rights I have listed. Do your own thinking. Do you have a permission to be you? Make your own list. Complete each of these phrases with ten different endings:

I have permission to be _____ .
I have permission to do _____ .
I have permission to have _____ .
I have permission to stop _____ .

When you take action from a position of power and choice you will leave guilt behind.

WHO DO YOU THINK YOU ARE?

Addictive eaters are usually all-or-nothing people. They tell themselves that they are only two choices: "either" and "or." I remember a compulsive overeater who was married for the second time and was having marital difficulties. She told me that when the going got rough between her and her husband, she could hear a little voice in her head saying, "Either eat or get a divorce." She chose food. Apparently it was the lesser of two evils. She had never considered that there were other alternatives such as marriage counseling. When she and her husband did go for counseling, they were able to resolve many of their conflicts.

When you limit yourself to only two choices and both are inadequate to solve your dilemma, you will feel stuck and continue to binge. Some of the polarities that binge eaters offer themselves are: either *good* or *bad*, either *perfect* or *failure*, either *attractive* or ugly, either *fat* or *thin*.

All-or-nothing thinking may be a long-time practice for you. Getting over it can become easier if you make it a game and laugh at yourself when you catch yourself instead of berating yourself for not being perfect.

Where did you get these irrational ideas that plague you and perpetuate unhappy feelings that trigger binges? The messages, both verbal and nonverbal, given by your parents when you were a small child constitute "commands." If you heard over and over again that you were a "difficult" child or that you were "a perfect angel," "Daddy's little pussycat," or "scatterbrained," you may still be acting in ways that justify that label. Your thoughts and ideas about yourself as a worthy person may even stem from the stories you were told about your birth.

Here is a checklist of questions that will enable you to understand who you think you are:

Personal Mythology

1. What were you told about your birth?
   Were you wanted? Were you an accident? Were you the preferred sex? Were your parents happy about your birth?
2. What were you told about the delivery?

Did Mother have a hard time or an easy time? Were you early or late or on time? As a result of your birth, you may be known for the rest of your life as "the pushy one who couldn't wait to be here" or "the lazy one who was two weeks late and took her time arriving." Were there complications during or after birth for you or your mother? Who was there? Did your father attend the birth?

3. What was happening in your family and their world at the time of your birth.

   Were your parents happy? Were there other children? How many? Were your parents having money or health problems at the time? What was going on in the world? Was it a time of peace and plenty or of war and scarcity?

4. What were you told about your infancy?

   Were you a "good" baby or troublesome? Did you have colic, allergies, illnesses? Did you cry too much? Did you eat too much or not enough? Were you breast-fed or bottle-fed? Who took care of you during your earliest years? How did your siblings feel about you?

5. What kind of personality or special traits did you have?

   Were you given nicknames because of your infancy? Were you labeled as the bright one, beauty, brains, rebel, devil, roly-poly, curious, too smart for her own good, friendly, or takes a lot of time and attention? Compare your labels with those given to your brothers and sisters. You will discover that all of them seem to be locked into a pattern of behavior that they have carried out throughout life. If you are the "baby," you may be treated as such even if you are fifty years old.

6. Take out photographs of yourself as a child.

   What memories do you recall as you look through your album? Compare what you remember with what you were told. Do your pictures agree with what your family told you about yourself? Often individuals who call themselves fat and ugly from childhood find out that they were adorable and normal but were labeled less than acceptable because they were compared with another sibling or because they had a personality or energy level that was considered unacceptable by the family.

Messages and commands were hidden within other messages. If you were told, "You're just like your father," you were being described as someone else saw you. It might have meant that you were a procrastinator like your father, a fussy eater, always sick, a go-getter, a born leader, a moody person, a compulsively neat person, or many other things. Who were you compared to? What were the qualities or traits that were implied? Do you agree today? Are you just like someone else in your family? In what ways are you different?

Frances told herself that she was just like her father. She had an irrational fear of being hungry. For the last forty years she had always eaten a snack before going out for dinner with her husband or friends. She feared that if she didn't eat, she would become dizzy and faint. She lived in constant fear that food would not be available. Car trips were interrupted with frequent stops for refreshments whether Frances was hungry or not.

It seemed that her father had behaved exactly the same way. Frances believed that it was a hereditary dysfunction. She was just like her father and had inherited his tendency to become ill after going without food. Like him, this obsession with food had lasted her entire adult life.

I asked Frances whether in all the years she had been worried about fainting she had in actuality ever become ill or fainted. She never had, but she was sure that was because she had taken good care of herself by eating before anything could happen.

She thought about the possibility that her father had not really been ill but only fearful. Perhaps her fear was not real but a product of what she was telling herself. She decided to tell herself that she could go for periods of time without eating because she was a normal human being. Perhaps her father had not actually been ill but once had eaten something that disagreed with him and had felt dizzy or ill and blamed it on the wrong reason.

Frances was tired of being enslaved by her irrational belief that she was just like her father. She decided to change. She told herself that she was a healthy woman who could eat three meals a day and go without snacks and not faint. She affirmed that she was not her father. She soon was able to take a five-hour car trip without stopping once for "refueling."

Your own view of the world and your part in it has to be looked at. Fear of intimate relationships and the inability to maintain a relationship are major problems for food abusers. One compulsive overeater, who is single, is torn between her desire to get married and raise a family and her belief that married people fight and live unhappily together (as her parents did for many years). She also tells herself that everyone she knows who was married is now divorced, so why should she bother. Yet she yearns to meet someone who will accept her unconditionally and want to be with her and be her best and most devoted friend. Every time she puts herself forward to meet men and does go out, she reacts by turning away through binges and an excuse to stay at home because of her weight gain.

The easiest way to uncover your life script messages and to evaluate them is to make a list of as many "shoulds" as you can. You may want to go back to this list again and again as new awarenesses come to you. Here are some suggested topics. Choose any that strike you as fitting. Under each write all the "shoulds" (or "wants me tos") that come to mind.

- A good person should, women should, men should, children should, mothers should, fathers should, lovers should, friends should, I should, brothers/sisters should
- My mother wants me to, my father wants me to, my spouse wants me to, my children want me to, my best friend wants me to, my boss wants me to, the government wants me to, my church wants me to, my neighbor wants me to
- Write the "shoulds" that go with each of these: Eating shoulds, diets shoulds, money shoulds (spending, saving, using), time shoulds (spending, using), sex shoulds, success shoulds, happiness shoulds, good manners shoulds, honesty and ethics shoulds

For each "should" you write, ask yourself who told you that—mother, father, teacher, sibling, or church. Then ask yourself if you are burdening yourself with guilt and anxiety in your efforts to carry out what you should be or do. If you are paying too much to satisfy someone else's belief, cross it out and replace it with your own belief about that same subject.

One of the beliefs that gives some food addicts trouble is, "Of course I love him; he is my father. You are supposed to love your father." When a person who has been beaten, insulted, sexually abused, or abandoned by a parent tries to talk herself into loving that person, she is left with enormous guilt for not being able to convince herself. My rule of thumb about relatives is to question whether, if that parent (or aunt or sister) were a neighbor of yours down the street, you would want to be his or her friend. I think that parents, like others, have to earn love. You may be able to show respect, but it is OK not to love an unlovable person. It is sometimes necessary to get a divorce from one or both of your parents to achieve peace of mind.

THOUGHTS ABOUT FEELINGS

There seem to be four basic feelings that trigger a binge: rejection, low self-worth, loneliness, and anger. These feelings can be avoided when the binger examines the underlying thoughts and changes them.

Rejection is a result of telling yourself that someone doesn't like you or want you. A friend who turns down a simple request because of another obligation may seem to be rejecting you, but is he? If a friend or fellow worker disagrees with you is that rejection? When your parents or spouse expect you to become responsible for your behavior or to become more independent, you may perceive that they are rejecting you and turning you out into the cold, cruel world, but they are really trying to help you to help yourself.

The more you tell yourself that you are being rejected because something is wrong with you, the more you will lose self-esteem. You will convince yourself that you are not a likable or capable person. If in your past you experienced poor parenting or little nurturing, you may expect everyone in your life today to give you what you missed out on. This expectation leads to the "bottomless pit" feeling. If you have binges during which, no matter how much you eat, you still feel empty, you are dealing with very old needs that have not been met and are projecting them onto a present-moment situation involving someone who was not responsible. No amount of food can fill that void, so stop trying and start to listen to your inner thoughts. If you are a perfectionist, you will be looking for ways to put yourself down and feel inadequate in comparison to others. What are you telling yourself? Is it the truth?

The same is true for feeling lonely. There is a big difference between loneliness and being alone. You may feel lonely in a crowd because you are telling yourself that you are not interesting to others, are stupid, ugly, or have such a "terrible secret" that you can't let anyone in on it or that person may hate you. The belief that you can't be happy unless there is someone else in your life, that you will be unfulfilled unless you have a mate, is not true. You can take care of your own needs and also have a partner in life, but that person doesn't have to be responsible for your happiness. Take that responsibility back and be in charge of your life by practicing the self-help program for change described in this book.

CHANGE TO POSITIVE THINKING

I have been describing all the ways food abusers hold beliefs that are destructive or untrue and lead to binges. Since thoughts trigger feelings and feelings seem like truth to most people, it is imperative to learn how to change your thoughts. There is a technique that is both simple and powerful. That is the use of self-affirmation. An affirmation is an emphatic statement. Although the word *affirm* means to declare positively, sometimes you may be declaring a negative view of yourself in a positive way, affirming that it is true. How many people constantly refer to themselves as someone who loses things, is poor in math, has a tin ear, or is unlucky? These are examples of affirming the negative.

A self-affirmation is a way to program your unconscious. The unconscious is like the genie of the magic lamp. In the story of Aladdin, when he rubbed the magic lamp, the genie appear and said, "I am the slave of the lamp. Your wish is my command." You see, genies must obey, no matter what. The unconscious is like that genie. It fulfills your commands, positive or negative. What you think about yourself often comes true. It is sometimes called a "self-fulfilling prophecy."

A self-affirmation means that you feed positive and healthy commands into your unconscious on purpose. You do it all the time without realizing it. If you decide that you need a new pair of shoes, you will find yourself looking into store windows, reading the ads in the paper for shoe sales, and thinking about the style, color, and price that are right. While you are looking and thinking, you never doubt that you will find the right shoes because you have had many pairs before and know that you deserve these shoes. You have gone through this process thousands of times in your life, choosing and expecting to achieve many goals, usually about material things such as clothing, cars, houses, and furniture. This same thinking pattern can work for you about health, relationships, happiness, and anything else you try it on.

When people start to work with affirmations, I suggest that they think up a simple positive statement—even a proverb or a prayer that will fit the bill. It has to be something that makes you feel good, that gives you a feeling of anticipation about how wonderful you will feel when this thought becomes reality for you.

Link the positive thought with a daily chore such as taking a bath or shower, setting the table, or driving to work. Say the self-affirmation out loud, quietly but firmly, ten times while you are doing the daily activity. Do this every day for at least a week. Some people prefer to write the affirmation ten times or more on a piece of paper. That is fine; just take one minute to focus on a positive thought. Just as your thoughts have led you to purchase a pair of shoes, your thoughts about feelings and relationships can lead you to what you really want.

Some self-affirmations that others have used are:

- I deserve the very best.
- I am lovable and capable.
- I choose to have a healthy body now.
- I am the master of my fate.
- I can be free of the bondage of food.
- New and loving friends are entering my life now.
- What others think about me is none of my business.
- What is to be is up to me.
- To change the world I find, I simply have to change my mind.

Please be sure to affirm for yourself. Do not attempt to manipulate others by affirming that someone else should shape up or start to love you. Look to yourself. What do you want most of all for yourself?

Saying self-affirmations out loud or writing them is easy to do and will become a daily habit. But not all the affirmations you choose will succeed. If any of your affirmations seem to stall, you must find out how you are stopping yourself by your negative thoughts or beliefs. The way to do this is simple. You will need a sheet of paper. Write your self-affirmation on the top. Say it out loud to yourself: "It's OK for me to make mistakes." Now say, "No, it isn't . . . " What is the critic within you telling you in rebuttal? It could be, "You make too many mistakes already" or "People will find out you aren't smart or talented." Perhaps your inner critic will explain, "That is not permitted in this family" or "You should know better." After each message from your critic, say the original positive self-affirmation out loud again and wait for the next barrage. Write down each negative argument. Keep this up until you have run out of reasons why you should not give yourself permission to have the positive and know you deserve it.

Here is an example:

Affirmation	Rebuttal
I am open to love now.	I am not aware of love. I'm cold. It's hard to respond to love.
I am open to love now.	I reject the love that comes to me because it is not the love I want.
I am open to love now.	I am afraid to allow love in. I don't understand how to let it flow.
I am open to love now.	I am afraid of being rejected if I let love in.
I am open to love now.	I am afraid of the responsibility love requires.
I am open to love now.	Love will weaken me. It will make me compromise.
I am open to love now.	I resist love because it will end, and I will be abandoned.
I am open to love now.	It will make me change. I am afraid to be changed.

The woman who wrote this list discovered that she was resisting love with all her might. She revealed to herself many fearful thoughts. None of these thoughts need to be true.

In this chapter I have suggested many ways for you to bring to light the ideas you have been hanging on to that lead to unhappiness and addictive eating. As you write each irrational or self-limiting thought, you will need to replace it with a new idea that you can and want to live with. To own the new thought and make it a part of the new you, write it down and look for the arguments that your critical self will put forth. Fight back and argue with this critical voice and you will soon feel comfortable with the new script that you are composing.

A wise person once said, "Stop living in the problem and start living in the answer." Eating disorders result from negative and destructive thinking patterns and the belief that they are true. To live in the answer, the binge eater can take a hint from the old song and "accentuate the positive" as well as "eliminate the negative."

RETRIEVING YOUR POWER

Almost every binge can be traced to a feeling of power-lessness over a situation or relationship. The food abuser is unable to cope with the frustration that arises when things don't go her way. The world is not as she would have it; her needs aren't being met; she hates herself and feels helpless to force herself to shape up; and it seems as if this state of affairs will go on eternally. I call this state of mind "Ain't it awful, and there's nothing I can do about it!"

I have already described the four-level plan for permanent change and have detailed the first three levels: physical, emotional, and intellectual. The fourth, the transpersonal level, is the most important. To change your life and eliminate eating disorders, you must know that no one else can do it for you. You must heal yourself. Often, as clients start to see the changes in themselves, as they become aware that they are acting and thinking in new ways—being assertive, feeling more confident, avoiding "dangerous" situations—they worry that the changes will fade and they will be unable to keep this new found health.

Recently, for example, a woman complained that she had tried to stay on a diet by making an oath to God. She thought that it would keep her "good" and was horrified when she continued to break her diet and her sacred oath.

When you have joined Weight Watchers or OA or gone to a diet doctor or nutritionist, did they send someone home with you to police your actions and make sure you didn't cheat? No! When you were good, who made you good? You did! How did you make yourself good? How can you continue to do the things you want in order to be free of the bondage of food?

YOUR INNER POWER

There is within each person an inner wisdom. You may have noticed that through the years you have helped others solve their problems, have taken over in emergencies, have been able to drive your car without accidents, have balanced your household budget, and have acquired friends who like you and think you are intelligent and interesting. How did you manage all of this? Within you is a storehouse of positive traits that have always been available. Some of you have used them more often and to better advantage than others. To change your eating behaviors, you will have to retrieve some of these powers and believe that they are available to you anytime, just like the many other powers you exercise every day without even thinking about them.

It's you who make a problem seem insoluble by your thoughts about it. You create the problem and keep it alive when you tell yourself that you don't know what to do. Here is a list of the tools that you have in your inner resource tool kit. The next time you feel stumped, sit down and write out what you are telling yourself about the situation. Then take a look at these qualities and find the ones that you need to use to change your thoughts and change the situation.

My Tools

admiration	faith	positiveness
appreciation	freedom	power
attention	friendship	promptness
beauty	generosity	quiet
bliss	goodness	reality
brotherhood	goodwill	renewal
calm	gratitude	resoluteness
compassion	harmony	serenity
cooperation	humor	service
courage	infinity	silence
creativity	initiative	simplicity
daring	integration	tenacity
decisiveness	joy	truth
detachment	liberation	understanding
determination	light	universality
discipline	love	vitality
endurance	order	wholeness
energy	patience	will
enthusiasm	peace	wisdom
eternity	persistence	wonder

III: A Self-Help Program for Change

After you have decided which qualities are needed, take some 3 x 5 cards and write the name of the quality in capital letters on each card. Hang these cards up next to the light switch in each room of your house. Each time you turn on the light, you will be reminding yourself of what you can do to change things.

Rhea was the only child of an aging and ailing mother. Rhea had her mother live with her because she didn't believe in nursing homes and thought she was doing her duty. Her mother's increasing infirmity was turning Rhea into a servant/nurse. She had to curtail her activities to take care of her mother. Her resentment was growing, and she was eating because of her feeling of powerlessness to change the situation. After all, there were no other relatives to help her. She simply couldn't see any solutions. This thought made her feel even more frustrated and locked in. When Rheas consulted the list of tools, she found that two words had the most meaning for her: compassion and initiative. She traded in her resentment for compassion and stopped hating her mother. She viewed the situation with love and understanding. Once she was free of anger, she used initiative to find out about getting trained aides to care for her mother to free herself and stop depriving herself of interests and activities she needed. This solution resulted in Rhea feeling good about her obligation and about herself.

Once you acknowledge that you do have many and varied positive traits and powers that can help you help yourself, you may wonder how to retrieve them when you need them.

Each human being perceives the world in three primary ways: visually, auditorily, and kinesthetically (touch and

222

sensation). Although we each use all these faculties, we each experience one mode that is dominant. Many people are used to understanding best from the printed word. They find that reading about things and writing down thoughts, as in a journal, help them get to the heart of the matter. Others are auditory and seem more comfortable with listening or hearing. An auditory person may prefer listening to music rather than watching TV. Sounds are important to these people. They may be happier thinking about things in their heads, rather than writing the words. Kinesthetic people do not primarily see or hear the answers but feel them as physical sensations like motion and muscle tension. Notice how many people say, "I had a feeling in my bones that something was wrong." Kinesthetic people have strong feelings of intuition and sense things in different parts of the body.

I recall talking one day with a client who was upset. As she talked, she kept swinging her foot. I asked her what her foot was saying. She translated the foot swing into a desire to kick. I pulled out a big, heavy floor pillow and asked her to kick it hard. As she kicked, I asked her what or whom she was angry about. She immediately spoke the name of the person she wanted to kick and was able to understand the cause of her conflict and deal with it.

Just as many people "feel" things on a body level, others see symbols or colors rather than words. (It is a shame that our schools and parents tell children that they are bad or lazy for daydreaming.) The creative imagination is a vital resource and a marvelous tool for change. Even if you were thwarted in developing your imagination in earlier times, you can reclaim this tool now.

III: A Self-Help Program for Change

Individuals who doubt their ability to express themselves in words may be able to capture feelings and thoughts through art. Pictures are indeed worth thousands of words to some. Occasionally, when I am counseling with someone, I will get a flash, a single picture or symbol about that person. I recall a session in which I had a sudden flash of a large stone fortress, such as was common in the Middle Ages. I asked my client if that image had meaning for him. He explained that he saw himself not only imprisoned within a fortress but locked into the highest tower. We were able to talk about how he put himself there and how and when he might be ready to get out. We looked for ways he might find allies to help end his feelings of isolation. The symbol became an analogy that led to new ideas and techniques.

In this chapter, I will suggest ways to retrieve your power. Some will involve words; many will be about symbols and imagery, some will ask you to create new methods and techniques through imagination. Kinesthetically oriented ideas will also be presented. Try them all and increase your repertoire of capabilities for growth.

CONTACTING YOUR WISE ADVISER

One of the first goals to achieve is to begin to know that you know more than you think you know. When you get up in the morning, you don't have to open your wallet to reassure yourself that you are male or female; nor do you have to refresh your memory about your name and address. You also have no doubts about certain of your skills. You know that you know how to read and write and do some mathematics. If you drive a car, ride a bicycle, speak a foreign language, or know how to type, you rarely have to prove your ability at that skill to yourself. The first step in learning to trust your inner wisdom is to practice making contact with it and finding out what it has to tell you.

The simplest way to meet and make friends with that wise self is to begin a correspondence. You may write a short letter to Wisdom just as you would write to "Dear Abby." You will find that it is more fun if you pick a real hero to address. Some of my clients have written to Jesus, Moses, George Washington, their grandfather, or Abby, among others. Write down one problem at a time, being specific and concrete in describing the difficulty. After you have completed the letter, take a new piece of paper and write an answer to yourself from Wisdom or your wise adviser. Don't try to figure out the answer; after all, you don't know it. Let your pen travel along, writing whatever comes to mind. After a few minutes you will discover that words start to flood onto the paper. Keep writing until you are through. Then read the second letter and think about the answer. Occasionally the critical self creeps in and dictates many "shoulds." If the answer from Wisdom seems to be reasonable and loving or easy to apply, you are on the right track. If the answer sets up a feeling of strong resistance, rewrite it and choose a different symbolic adviser.

When I wanted to write my first book, I sat down to put my ideas on paper, but I couldn't seem to get started. The book was based on a series of classes that I had been teaching for five years. All the information was in my head just bursting to come out. I tried speaking into a tape recorder and then typing the result, but it was terrible. Finally, I decided to ask for help. I wrote a letter to someone I admire for his creativity, wit, and warmth: Steve Allen. I told him about my problem and asked for a solution. Then I took a new piece of paper and wrote Steve's answer to me. The solution was almost too easy. I was told to take my outline and label a number of manila folders with each main topic. Then I was to sit at my typewriter and start typing. Whatever I wrote was then to go into the proper folder. I had no objections to giving the method a try. It worked. I began to type, and the book seemed to write itself.

The nice thing about writing to your symbolic adviser is that you can find out answers to difficult problems immediately, especially if you aren't near a phone or your therapist is unavailable. The answer is inside you, and only you have access to it. The more you practice consulting yourself, the more certain you will be that you do know what you need to do and how to do it.

If you hate to write, sit down in a comfortable chair and close your eyes. Put yourself in a lovely meadow, on a mountaintop, or in a pleasant private room that you conjure up in your imagination. Then call your inner wise friend to join you and hold a conversation with her or him. Tell him what is troubling you and listen for his answer. If you don't get a suitable reply, call someone else to you. You can choose anyone you want for your imaginary consultation.

When you trust that your wisdom is always within and available, you can think up your own unique system. One man I know, who works for a large corporation, pretends that he is sitting in front of a computer. He imagines the keyboard and types his problem into the machine. He requests an answer and gives the computer a specific order for the day and time he needs to have the solution. Then he relaxes and knows that the computer is working on the task. He usually does this before going to sleep and orders the answer for the next morning. And he get the answer!

Your body is a wondrous machine. Too many bingers deny the wisdom of their bodies. Conversing with parts of the body, either in your imagination or on paper, will give you some surprises. The bulimics who want to be empty and stay empty are afraid of their digestive tracts. Talking to your stomach or your intestines may reveal fears you have been avoiding. Once a woman complained of a sharp pain in her heart in the midst of a session. She felt panicked and feared she was suffering a heart attack. I asked her to interpret the pain and ask her heart what it was telling her. She learned that she was afraid to be alone.

Have you even considered having a conversation with your problem—anorexia, bulimia, or overeating? Find out what your eating disorder wants to say to you. Pretend that you are a TV interviewer and make up a list of questions to ask your disorder. Go down the list and write out the answers as they come to you. Here are some of the frequently asked questions? Why won't you go away? What do you get out of making me miserable? How can I stop you? What am I afraid will happen when I do get rid of you?

III: A Self-Help Program for Change

YOU CAN DRAW YOUR ANSWERS

Turning your thoughts and feelings into pictures may put an entirely different slant on things. Get some crayons and draw compulsion. What color and shape is it? Draw how you feel when you binge. Draw a binge. Draw a design that expresses how you want to become. Hang it up where you can look at it. Think about the qualities you will need to overcome your eating problem. Draw a design or picture of love, power, or whatever trait you need. If you become upset but can't seem to identify the feeling or thought that is triggering the binge, draw how you feel before you begin to binge.

Symbols are a fascinating shorthand to help you gain awareness and understanding. You may get a symbol in a dream or it may come to you when you relax and close your eyes. Ask your creative imagination to give you a symbol for a specific situation or relationship. Make a picture of the symbol. Then take a piece of paper and write a note from the symbol to you.

Leah was upset over her teenage daughter's relationship with a boy friend. Many of Leah's binges were linked to her feelings of disappointment and frustration that her daughter wasn't listening to her advice. Leah asked her inner wisdom to give her a symbol to help resolve the problem. Leah saw a key in her imagination. I asked her to write, "I am the key and I have something to tell you..." A few minutes later Leah looked up from her writing to share that she now realized that she was the "key" to the problem. She put herself and her feelings between her daughter and the boy friend. She made the problem for herself. She vowed to stop meddling. She decided to let her daughter work out her own problems.

USE YOUR IMAGINATION

Over the years, I have learned that most people don't think they know their own answers—but they do. I know that you know, and I can help you find out how much of your wisdom is untapped. One technique that I often suggest is one I call the "Automatic Teller Machine in the Sky." When you use an ATM, you follow a three-step procedure:

1. You enter your code and ask for a response (either a withdrawal or deposit receipt).
2. You stand and wait, knowing that the wise teller machine is taking care of your business.
3. The machine returns your cash or receipt.

The three-step technique for problem solving is similar:

1. On a sheet of paper write a question about yourself—a personal problem to which you have no inkling of the answer.
2. Read the question out loud and send it off to the "cosmic teller." Close your eyes and relax. You don't have to know the answer, but you have to be ready to receive it in a quiet state.
3. You will receive the answer in one of three ways: a word or thought, a flash of a picture or shape, or

a strong feeling or sensation in your body. Write or draw your answer under your question.

Then start again using the answer as a jumping-off point. If your answer is true, what would you want to find out next? Keep asking questions and receiving answers until you feel finished.

Darla asked the "cosmic teller" why she had a compulsion to eat from other people's plates. The answer was a picture of her mother. Her next question was, "What does my mother have to do with my problem?" She received the information that her mother was always commenting on how much she ate, so Darla, as a child, decided that what she ate from others' dishes didn't count and could miss her mother's watchful eyes.

Cathleen couldn't figure out why she was binging almost daily between noon and two in the afternoon. When she asked her question, she received a picture of a restaurant she frequented when she lived in another city. Further questioning revealed that she often lunched there on business. She enjoyed the atmosphere and the socializing of a business lunch. Cathleen now works at a job at which she is alone between noon and two. She realized that she was eating to recreate the nice feelings she had in the old days.

When you receive an answer that puzzles you, just ask the "cosmic teller" for the interpretation. This is a no-fault system. You can't help but get answers to your questions, so be persistent.

Our language is filled with symbolism and metaphor. We constantly make word pictures to aid in communicating. Pretty as a picture, sick as a dog, jump with joy, and bright as a penny are common expressions. We often tell others that we're going to "clean up our act." Cleaning up and cleaning out old ideas and habits can become a ritual like spring cleaning. When you clean out your emotional closet, you can make room for new, healthy, and successful ideas and experiences. Are you ready to let go of worn-out ideas, worn-out conditions, and worn-out relationships?

Make a list of all the old ideas about food, eating habits, purging behavior, weight loss and gain, social expectations, lovability, and anything else that comes to mind. Then make a list of the conditions in your life that you wish you could change such as lack of money, trouble with career, compulsion to eat or purge, or beliefs that no one will love you if you aren't perfect to look at. What relationships are the most difficult for you? Make a list of old and new relationships that you would like to change.

Take each worn-out object/idea from your list and ask yourself if you are truly sick and tired of having it. If any "yes but . . ." thoughts flit across your mind, write them down for further consideration.

Making a ceremony of the ordinary act of throwing out unneeded or unwanted stuff is an effective way to retrieve your power. Write every old belief, condition, or relationships that you are ready to be free of on a slip of paper and throw each one away or burn it after you have announced, "I don't need you anymore. I don't want you anymore." In days to come, if one of these old thoughts recurs, remind yourself that you no longer think or act this way. The past is past, and you are free of it.

III: A Self-Help Program for Change

PERSONAL RITUALS AND RITES

Each culture and each family has rituals that enrich life. Each of our holidays is filled with activities that we enjoy. Religious or cultural observances mark the rites of passage from childhood to adult status. New Year's Eve is a letting go of the past and welcoming the new year. You can reinforce new ideas and work toward achieving your goals by making up your own rituals to mark your progress.

When I moved into my present home, the house was hard to get used to. It seemed to contain an aura of the family who had previously lived in it. After a few months of uneasiness, I had a combination housewarming and exorcism party to take formal ownership and get rid of the "ghosts" in the house. Fortunately, I have a magic wand which I find helpful on such occasions. During the party, each guest was invited to wave the wand and bless the house. After the party, I felt really comfortable and at home at last.

One memorable ritual I shared with a client named Jessica involved her desire to get rid of the burden of her past. She wanted to make room in her life for new experiences and learn new ways to react to stress. Together, we decided to let her die to the old and be reborn. So we held a mock funeral. Jessica invited a few of her closest friends. Each one gave a eulogy praising her for her strong positive traits. Before the ceremony, Jessica and I had compiled a list of the worn-out ideas that she wanted to be rid of. During the funeral, these ideas were ceremonially destroyed.

Immediately afterward there was a rebirth ceremony in which Jessica was welcomed back. Each friend presented her with a special gift to mark the event and acted like a fairy godmother, using the magic wand to share blessings of the spirit. General rejoicing followed. It was a reminder to Jessica that the event marked her commitment to change. She was "dead" to her old ways and her old consciousness but would continue to incorporate new and healthy ways of dealing with her life problems.

A ritual I have fantasized but not yet carried out would involve attaching pieces of paper on which you write your worn-out ideas or resentments to the tail of a kite. This activity would be fun as a group outing. Each person could share what she is letting go of. Then each would fly the kite and let go of the string. A variation of this theme would be to use balloons and let them go in a huge bouquet. What fun!

CHANGING BAD FEELINGS FOR GOOD

Change doesn't have to be solemn or painful. Using your creativity and imagination plus a dash of humor, you can come up with some wonderful experiences to celebrate your healing. I suggest some simple but uplifting techniques for projecting yourself into the future you want. It has been said that "what man can conceive, man can achieve." If you can't form a dream or vision, you will have trouble achieving the positive goal.

One of my favorite activities for predicting/creating the future is to make a scrapbook. You can do this alone or with a group of friends. All you need is some notebook paper, scissors, tape, and lots of old magazines. Pick one goals you want to achieve. Don't be worried about how or when it will happen; this is a fantasy, so you don't have to be concerned. You may choose a specific topic like being free of the bondage of food or having a good love relationship, prosperity, good health, a trip, or peace of mind.

Go through the magazines without talking. Look for words and pictures that reflect your goal. Keep your thoughts focused on the goal. When you have a pile of words and pictures, paste them on the sheets of paper and make a book. As you leaf through the book, you will be surprised to find how your energy changes. You will feel happy and excited as you imagine having the things you want. Keep looking through your scrapbook from time to time to remind yourself that you can have what you want.

Another way to experience the good feelings of change is to have a "party of the future." Invite a few friends to join you for a party. Before you start, have each one share something about his or her life that is limiting and unsuccessful. Have each friend tell the fantasy of what he or she would like that area of life to be. Have everyone hold hands and pretend that time is passing. You may want to count off the seconds as if they were years. When you open your eyes, pretend that ten years have passed and that each one has achieved his goal and is meeting once again. Have a real party, but make believe that you are the successful person you want to be. You might even make little award certificates or have toy trophies to share. Each person can be called forth to receive a token of success. Use your imagination and see what happens. I guarantee that you will feel very "high" on your positive thoughts.

Since most binge eaters tend to think negatively of themselves, this technique may remind you that things aren't always as bad as you think they are. Start a "cookie jar" but without cookies. Every time someone writes you a sweet personal note or special card, put it into your cookie jar. You can buy a decorative canister or use an old cigar box, but keep all the good thoughts in one place. Remember the handmade cards that your children made for Mother's Day or birthdays. Put anything and everything that can remind you that you are indeed lovable and worthy into this container. When you feel depressed and low, take out your "cookies" and tell yourself that they represent the truth about you. These messages can cheer up a rainy day or a day after a binge.

JOURNALS AND DREAMS

Fantasy can be a new and exciting tool to learn to use. A more down-to-earth approach to help you understand yourself and believe in your capabilities is journal writing. In the last few years, a number of books and classes have been made available to the public to teach the art of psychological journal writing. If you want to keep track of your thoughts and feelings in an ongoing manner, that is fine. Getting your feelings out and your ideas down in black and white can relieve extreme tension and help you see things more objectively. One quick rule that I have found to be successful is to complete your writing and then reread it. Next, answer these two questions:

1. What did I just discover from reading my journal entry?

2. What action can I take to change things for the better? (Can I change what I tell myself or can I change something about the situation or relationship?)

Keeping dream journals is also a way that many people learn to help themselves. Your dreams come from within you. They are messages from you to you. But you must learn how to decode them. Again, a multitude of excellent books are available for guidance. Many therapists will work with your dreams, and some will help you to act them out. You might draw pictures about them or share them in groups. As you trust your dream power, you will feel more able to direct your unconscious to give you answers while you sleep.

One simple method for beginning to learn about dreams is to write down whatever you remember from your dreams for about a month. Don't try to analyze them. After you have collected a large number of entries, read through them from start to finish. You may get the message immediately.

This happened to Florence. She kept having dreams about ladies' rooms—not bathrooms or toilets—ladies' rooms! Florence didn't have the same dream over and over, but she had many dreams that took place in ladies' rooms. She was embarrassed to discuss it and couldn't understand what each dream was about. When she had collected a month's worth of dreams and read through them, she suddenly became aware that the dreams reflected her desire to overcome her fears of independence. She needed to find her place in the world. The ladies' rooms symbolized giving herself room as a capable and talented woman (lady). The dreams reassured her that she was grappling successfully with her desire to be whole and able to take care of herself as a working woman.

Some wonderful journal writing ideas can help you finish unfinished business from your past. Although an important person from your life may be dead or far away, you can write your thoughts or even have dialogues to discuss the remnants of anger or hurt that you are still carrying with you.

Don't forget creative writing as a means of self-expression. Try your hand at poetry or story writing. Perhaps you can write a song or even a play. Since so much writing is autobiographical, you might write the story of your life. One client found that she learned best when writing about herself in the third person. Instead of saying, "When I was a child . . ." she wrote, "Once there was a girl named Cynthia. She lived with her parents . . ."

Whether you write in a serious mode or make fun of yourself, give writing a chance.

FANTASY AND RELAXATION

Corinne refused to write a food diary, any journal entries, or a homework assignment, no matter how small. She said she had no time or energy because she was on twenty-four-hour guard duty, making sure she protected herself from her own weaknesses and fears about the world. Corinne saw herself as a one-woman army with no allies or reinforcements to give her time to relax and regroup.

Dieters, especially bulimics and anorectics, have a widespread attitude that there is something wrong with the body and they must get it to work right. They do not trust themselves or their internal organs. I was trying to reassure Teri that she had a marvelous body and could think of it as an ally. I reminded her that most people don't wake up in the middle of the night to make sure their lungs are working and they are breathing. Teri said that she did. What a burden to have to make yourself responsible for everything in your body, both physical and emotional, twenty-four hours a day. No wonder some bulimics and anorectics are tense!

But what if you do have an ally, a helper that you can trust? The creative unconscious is that friend. Your unconscious is a vast storehouse of memories and ideas. You can order your inner self to reveal information and to help you. One way to achieve a respite from frantic worrying is to use meditation and guided fantasy techniques. You will be able to give yourself time to feel calm while you let your imagination and your unconscious go to work. As you practice these new skills, you will gain a feeling of trust in yourself and your body.

Perhaps you need only to relax. One simple fantasy that you can practice is to imagine yourself in a quiet and beautiful, safe place. Concentrate on the beauty of your surroundings. Let down your guard and relax. You may want to listen to soft music to get in the mood to float and feel happy.

A favorite fantasy of mine is the trip down "Memory Lane." Sit comfortably and close your eyes. Let your thoughts take you back through your life as you relive the happiest moments. Make sure you look only for the *positive* memories. Remember friends from your childhood, parties, pets, trips, beautiful scenery, triumphs, secret joys.

Get into the feelings of happiness as you take time out from your worries.

You can also take a "Magical Mystery Tour" by choosing a lyrical piece of music, closing your eyes, and letting the music take you somewhere. You may know where you want to go or you can pretend to see a door and go through it to somewhere that surprises you. In your imaginary travels, you may find some answers to your problems.

I have been told that the genius Mozart used to have his wife read out loud to him from a novel while he composed. He said that it distracted him, so he could let the music flow through him. When you focus on your limitations, doubts, and fears, you close the channel to your own divine "music" or wisdom. Let go and let your cares float away like little toy boats gliding down the stream. As you relax, many insights can come into your awareness. Stop trying so hard to make things happen!

FAITH, THE INVISIBLE STRENGTH

If you feel that you must always be in charge of your life and responsible for change, yet you aren't able to succeed in overcoming your problems, you may want to consider one of the most potent tools for change ever known: faith. A minister I know frequently chides people who are stuck in their problems, "Don't you have an invisible means of support?"

Some people have turned their backs on their religious upbringing because it was too dogmatic or negative. If you are one of those, you need to know it is not necessary to

239

believe in God as you were taught. You may find a new alternative. But if you believe in something on a spiritual level, you can harness this divine energy to overcome your eating problem. It is not necessary to belong to a specific religion or to attend church. All that is necessary is to tap into whatever you do believe and make it work for you and with you every day.

There is a wonderful story often told in Alcoholics Anonymous about two prospectors in the Yukon who were arguing over the existence of God. One maintains that there is a God, while the other says he has proof that there is no God. "How can you prove there is no God?" "Well," says the doubter, "I was out hunting and got lost in a blizzard. The snow erased the trail. I thought I was a goner. I got down on my knees and prayed. 'God, if there is a God, please help me now.'" "But you are here," said the believer. "That proves there is a God." "Naw," said the doubter. "Some damn Eskimo came and showed me the way home."

Perhaps you can think of the "Eskimos" in your life. You don't have to do it all yourself. There are others who can lead you to a new place. Maybe you will meet them if you join a support group. Telling a friend or trusted relative about your problem may help you get "home" to health.

It is not hard to turn to your faith to help you. Alicia, a young adult with a compulsive eating problem, was distraught because her alcoholic father was making demands upon her to live her life to please him. Alicia wanted to quit college and work. When she told her father of her decision, he threatened to kill himself. Alicia felt blackmailed. She was brought up to believe that you must honor your father and mother. Every day she fought with her guilt and fear. If she did what she wanted, perhaps she would be responsible for his death. She couldn't find a way to please herself and her father.

Evelyn lived according to a script her mother had prescribed for her. Her mother often warned Evelyn that if she gave up her career to get married, she would be a failure, fat and miserable, destined to die young. Evelyn married to escape her mother, gave up her career, and gained seventy-five pounds. She dropped out of life and began to abuse alcohol and drugs. She felt sure she was killing herself and would die young just as her mother predicted.

Both Alicia and Evelyn had a profound faith in God. But they had made their parents their gods. I asked each of them to perform a special ritual each morning. When they arose, they were to give the troublesome parent to God. After all, neither woman was powerful enough to change the problem parent or to help the parent see things in a different light. Since each trusted God and knew that God was more powerful, she was willing to try this new idea.

Evelyn decided to light a candle and surround her mother in light while commending her to the great and loving power. With the burden of trying to please a frightening mother authority figure removed, Evelyn could get on with her life. She eventually lost most of her excess weight, gave up on drugs and alcohol, and began a new and loving relationship with her mother after years of bitterness.

Alicia also gave her father to God. She had to keep reminding herself that if he did indeed harm himself, it was not her fault. As she refused to feel guilt, she was able to stand up to her father and assert herself. The knowledge and practice of her own power helped her to reduce her binges. She was no longer a victim but someone who knew that she deserved the very best.

If there is someone in your life who controls you through emotional blackmail, give this person to God. One way to practice not being your loved one's keeper is to conjure up a guardian angel for him or her. Turn your loved one over to the care of this divine helper or write a letter to the guardian angel asking for help.

Bridget had been having treatment with a Christian counselor who assigned her to read specific passages in the Bible that related to her problems. Bridget ate because of her family problems—a husband who had a terrible temper and two rebellious teenage sons. She found comfort by using the Bible as a resource.

One of the best affirmations for Bridget came from Ephesians 6:13, "the whole armor of God." Every morning she would read the passage that explained that the armor of God suggests protection to those who believe. Bridget would imagine herself putting on the "breastplate of righteousness," the "shield of faith," and the "sword of the Spirit." Thus girded, she could face the trials and tribulations of the day. As she continued to use her faith, she felt stronger and stronger. She began to give up her role as victim. She spoke up to her husband and children, demanded respect, and gained respect for herself by giving herself quiet times for prayer and times for her own needs. The more she was able to fill her needs, the fewer binges she had.

Another tool that Bridget used was to give love. She wrote letters to her husband and her children from time to time telling them about the qualities she appreciated in them or thanking them for something they had said or done. When she centered herself in love and not fear, she felt less resentment and stress and avoided many temper tantrum binges.

FORGIVENESS

Forgiveness is a tool that will help you cleanse and heal many open wounds that plague you. To practice forgiveness is very difficult because many binge eaters carry around grudges and are unwilling to write them off until they have received what is owed: love, apologies, caring, approval. You hurt yourself by constantly reminding yourself of how others have failed you and what they should give you.

Make a list of people in your life, past and present, who have not lived up to your expectations or whom you are angry at or afraid of. For each name, write the specific deed or situation that you have not forgotten or forgiven. Be aware of how much energy it takes to keep your anger going and how it depletes you. Think how good and how light you will feel when you release the other person.

When you are ready to let go of the old grudges, set a specific time and place to celebrate forgiveness. If you want, invite a special friend and make the ceremony into a celebration. Say out loud the name of the person you forgive and what it is that you forgive him or her for doing, or saying, or for not doing or saying.

After Jill released her former husband because he hadn't paid child support for five years, she felt renewed. A week later, he called and told her that conditions were suddenly improving in his life. She explained that she had just let go of her anger toward him. He said, "Your hold on me was very great!" He also began to pay child support.

Now you need to forgive yourself. Write down all your misdemeanors. What are your major faults or sins? Have you realized that in modern society even murderers can get out of prison on parole after a few years? Yet food addicts condemn themselves to lifelong purgatory!

Look at your list of offenses toward yourself and others. Think of the person you love most in the world. If this were his or her list, could you forgive him or her? Make a special time for your personal forgiveness ceremony. You may want to say a prayer or recite a poem to set the mood. Read each item on your list and announce out loud that you forgive yourself. Then tear up or burn your list.

Meditation is another effective tool for change. Some people are afraid to meditate because they think they will not do it "right." Not all meditation takes place in a cross-legged sitting position. You may want to read a book or take a class about meditation techniques. Meditation is a single-focus activity. Meditation is being fully conscious in whatever state you are—right now. It is possible to meditate while you are sewing or gardening or playing a musical instrument. The important thing is to stay in the *now* moment; be aware when your mind wanders, and return to total awareness of what's going on at this moment. You experience a vacation from care when you are absorbed in an activity you enjoy. Practice it often.

There is no danger from "overdoing" this meditation because you do it when you intend to.

Other meditation techniques involve the use of a mantra or phrase or sound that is recited over and over. You can invent your own mantra in the form of a proverb or favorite inspirational phrase such as, "The Lord is my shepherd," or "Be still and know that I am." Take some time away from your obsessional thoughts and worries about binge eating to place your consciousness in a peaceful and positive place. You will experience change in a surprisingly short time.

THE POWER OF YOUR UNCONSCIOUS MIND

You will not be able to retrieve your power unless you believe that you have the power to help yourself. Although groups, classes, and individual counseling will facilitate change, total healing will come through you. The more you give yourself the opportunity to learn how to get in touch with the great resources within you and your own inner wisdom, the easier it will become to know what to do.

It is a commonly held belief that under hypnosis a person can regress to a moment in childhood and describe in great detail the design of the rug on the floor, the activities taking place, and the words and feelings being expressed. This means that every experience you've ever lived is stored within. Think of your unconscious as a large library filled with millions of microfilmed moments. Be confident that by using some of the methods I have described, you can have access to all that you need. The raw materials for success are waiting for you. Only you can know when to act and how to put it all together.

The most important thing to keep in mind is *don't give up!* I remember a woman who took my behavior modification class many years ago. She showed up every week but slept through the entire class. After the first semester was completed, she signed up for Part Two and slept through that one, too. Three years later she called me and asked if I remembered her. I certainly did! She told me that she was too threatened by the class and couldn't deal with her fears, so she turned away in sleep. Yet the few things she did allow herself to hear had remained, and she was ready to start again. She continued to attend my classes and stayed awake. She committed herself to keep working on her fear and resistance to eliminating binge eating. Although it is still an on-again-off-again battle, she is now determined to keep on until she wins.

If you aren't ready to work the four-level plan today, you can become ready. You can begin with a letter to your wise adviser asking how to help yourself begin. Or you can practice calling on your "cosmic teller." If you take only one step toward positive change, it will lead to the next and the next.

Remember that working the four-level plan can change your life. If you find yourself resisting, think about why you want to hang on to your problem. Only when you are "sick and tired of being sick and tired" will you change. I like to use this formula for change: *When the pain of what you are doing outweighs the pleasure you get from doing it, you will change.*

Perhaps you have decided that you don't want to wait until the pain of your problem becomes overwhelming.

You may still be afraid that you will have to give up too much to overcome your eating disorder. That is a fantasy. You will not have to give up food, but you do need to give up food abuse. You will not have to give up friendship or love, but you will need to give up fear of rejection, loneliness, and guilt. Change doesn't have to be painful; it's fighting change that usually hurts.

The plan for permanent change is simple though it isn't always easy. First, you will learn to change your behavior by becoming willing to observe and take responsibility for what you do with food. Keep in mind that a binge is a signal of inner conflict. Binging doesn't mean you are a bad person. Second, you must learn that binges and purges represent intense, unexpressed feelings. Learn to know what feelings you are hiding from yourself and others. Sometimes the feeling is hunger because you may be dieting or fasting to the point of starvation. Third, you can change what you think. My rule of thumb is to ask, "Does this belief or idea help me or hurt me?" If it detracts from your success or health, you can evaluate and rewrite it. As you practice self-awareness of your inner monologue, you will change your world from one of negativity and doubt to one of hope and health. Fourth, know and trust in yourself as a lovable and capable human being, one who deserves the very best.

This plan is not meant to be used the way a diet is—employed for a few weeks and then discarded. The four-level plan is a plan for total and permanent change. It will take constant vigilance to monitor your thoughts, feelings, and actions. You already have this ability. Since food addicts are usually obsessed with self-judgment and sometimes spend most of every day observing and wrestling with negative and compulsive behavior, this plan offers a new way to expend the same energy and get results. Instead of giving in to irrational beliefs about yourself as a weak and hateful person, you can retrain your attitudes and teach yourself a set of skills for eliminating binge eating from your life. Only you can decide if it is worth the time and effort to trade your misery for a life of freedom from the bondage of food.

IV

Food for Thought

HOW PSYCHOTHERAPY CAN HELP

Many food abusers have benefited from psychotherapy by overcoming related psychological problems such as depression, trouble with relationships, and fears. Although they gained insight and the ability to solve problems, they did not eliminate the eating problem. A professional with experience treating eating disorders will be able to work with both the inappropriate eating behavior and the related psychological issues.

Three types of therapy are available: talk therapy, body work therapy, and creative arts therapy. Most people imagine that going for therapy means sitting or lying down and talking to someone who either listens and nods or talks back to you, discussing what you have related, sometimes interpreting or explaining, other times challenging. There are many types and styles of talk therapy. Most involve helping people to talk about the problems they are unable to solve. Some are self-probing and analytical. Transactional analysis and cognitive therapy are strongly educational. In talk therapy, there is a verbal interaction between the client and the therapist. Through discussion and insight, the client learns to make new choices, change attitudes, and rehearse new behaviors.

There are body work therapies such as rolfing, bioenergetic, and neo-Reichian therapy. These modes arose from the belief that the entire body contains the recorded effects of life experiences that can replay as feelings and memories. Much energy and many feelings can be imprisoned in muscles habituated through years of restraint and posture control. This control is often the cause of specific body types and chronic body tensions.

All the body work therapies attempt to unblock the flow of energy in the body by unknotting tensions caused by past experiences. By improving the body tone and posture and exploring the body consciousness, a total mind and body change can take place.

Creative arts therapies are experiential activity processes that are sometimes nonverbal. Creative activities help you to find understandings and solutions "beyond words." Creative arts therapy may involve art, music, dance, body movement, poetry, dreams, and other creative processes. Guided fantasy or "mind trips" as well as hypnosis are included in this category. The common factor in all these techniques is that they all encourage right-brain activity. The right brain is thought to be the gateway to intuitive, creative expression as contrasted to the left-brain activities, which relate to logic and words, math, and the majority of everyday experiences in our culture.

You do not have to have any talent in art, music, or dance to benefit from and enjoy the therapy. You do not have to think about what is happening; by doing it, you are working through conflicts and resolving problems.

GROUP THERAPY

Group therapy is one of the most successful forms for food abusers. Whether you participate in a leaderless support group, a non-professional self-help group such as Over-eaters Anonymous, or a group led by a professional therapist, you will discover that the experience can be very beneficial.

An expression often heard in a group therapy session is, "I always thought I was the only person who ever felt this way." The realization that you are not alone is one of the many benefits of group experience. Other advantages include group support for risk taking, feedback from different perspectives, and a group laboratory for ex-perimenting with new social behaviors. Witnessing others struggling to resolve life issues can powerfully motivate you to tackle tasks that you once thought impossible. Most people can gain courage and confidence faster working in a group than in a one-to-one therapy setting.

Over the years, compulsive overeaters have flocked to diet clubs, classes, and doctors. Overeaters have little fear of being together, but anorectics and bulimics are extreme-ly secretive. This reluctance to come out can hinder them from finding the help they desperately want. Self-help groups or therapy groups offer friendship and acceptance. The first step to overcoming binge eating is to be able to accept yourself as a worthwhile person. When you come to a group and see people with eating disorders who are attractive, intelligent, creative, and lovable, you may be able to give up the sense of alienation that keeps you stuck in your own circular, self-deprecating thinking.

Self-help groups can also be inspirational. A newcomer can hear success stories of others who were caught in the compulsion of binging, purging or starving and are now free of these habits. The most available self-help group for people with food addictions is Overeaters Anonymous.

A great many food abusers come from families of alcoholism or depression. Al Anon, Codependents Anonymous, and Adult Children of Alcoholics (and Trauma) are other worthwhile free support groups they can benefit from. Emotional Health Anonymous is a twelve step group which helps people deal with out of control emotions. Recovery is a different type of self-help organization which has been in existence for many years helping people deal with debilitating emotional problems, especially depression. Since most self-help groups are non-profit and are no cost or very low cost, there is little reason not to get help when it is reasonable and available.

THE ROLE OF A THERAPIST

Some people think that going to a therapist is like going to a care mechanic: they expect the therapist to diagnose a specific problem and fix it just as the mechanic puts in new brake pads or readjusts the carburetor. These clients expect something to happen to them. This is not the case.

13: HOW PSYCHOTHERAPY CAN HELP

A psychotherapist helps you to discover answers inside yourself: your thoughts, feelings, perceptions, and belief systems. There also may be answers to be found outside yourself in the form of resources, people, and even events in your everyday world. In the course of seeking these answers, the therapist may provide you with much needed experiences for learning to relate to others and the world around you through action, drama, communications, and even colors and images. Therapists have no "shots" to give you, but they do have skills that they teach and share with you, so that you may decrease the difficulties in your life and increase the benefits. Do not expect any other person to have all the answers. You have the answers, and the therapist is there to help you retrieve them from within yourself.

When a client comes into my office and tells me of her problem, if I believe in the problem as much as she does, I cannot help her. I have to know the truth about each person I see. The truth is that each individual is a perfect person who has the capacity to be strong and wise. Each one is capable and lovable but doesn't know it. The client has "blind spots" that prevent her from seeing the total picture. I can see the situation with more objectivity and point out the "blind spots." I can see that the problem has grown from stumbling blocks the person has put in her own path and from inadequate skills or lack of information.

Sometimes a client is trying to solve a problem with the wrong set of tools. This is especially true of bulimics. The bulimic starts out by using purging as the answer to her problem of how to eat a lot and stay slim. What starts as an answer eventually becomes a problem. The bulimic continues to use binge/purge behavior to resolve anxiety. She is using the wrong materials. I can help by pointing this out and by helping her decide on different resources she can gather to deal with the stresses in her life.

There are many types of therapy to choose from. Find the one that is right for you. Some therapists combine many modalities in their work. Be sure to work with someone you can trust. If you will not or cannot tell your therapist that you vomit, you will not be able to help yourself stop. If you are working with someone you do not like or trust, you may need to shop around until you find someone you feel good about. It is your money and time that you are spending. The public gives great power to doctors and therapists, yet they are only human and therefore imperfect.

HOW TO CHOOSE THE RIGHT THERAPIST

You may have decided that it is time to ask for help in overcoming your eating disorder. Most people have no sound basis for choosing the right therapist or doctor. Since many therapists are trained to practice a particular type of therapy, you will get what that person knows best. But it may not be what is best for you. There are many psychotherapists who are like general practitioners, dealing with a little of everything. They may have attended a few classes or workshops about eating disorders, but they do not keep up with the literature or see many cases. I advise you to find a therapist who spends over 50% of his or her time treating eating disorders. Your therapist may be a psychiatrist, social worker, marriage counselor, pastoral counselor or psychologist.

Here are some guidelines to help you choose:

1. The therapist specializes in eating disorders.
2. The therapist asks you to have a medical evaluation with a blood electrolyte panel for bulimics and anorectics.
3. The therapist refers you for nutritional consultation at some point in your treatment.
4. The therapist admits limitations and doesn't pretend to know things he or she doesn't know.
5. The therapist continues to read in the field of specialization and goes to trainings, workshops or conferences for continued education.
6. The therapist says things that make sense to you.
7. The therapist answers your direct questions.
8. The therapist is willing to see significant people who share your life as part of your recovery process.
9. The therapist acts as your consultant rather than a judgmental parent.

Even if your therapist or doctor has many degrees and letters after his or her name, if you do not feel comfortable with him, find someone else! Some food addicts prefer therapists with a dynamic personality, while others feel reassured with someone who is more low-key. You may prefer a male or female. You will know if you are recovering because after a short time, you will feel more hopeful, begin to see changes in your behavior, and have a higher self-esteem.

A TOTAL PROGRAM FOR RECOVERY

No amount of psychotherapy will cure you of low potassium caused by purging. The most effective approach combines psychological, dietary and medical treatment. All sufferers of addictive eating problems need to be evaluated by a doctor who has had experience dealing with food related problems and knows how to look for electrolyte imbalances, malnutrition, hypoglycemia, depression, and other physiological illnesses that may be causing the problem with food or that are the result of purging or starving.

A trained eating disorder specialist will also refer you to a qualified nutritionist to identify and change your chaotic or restrictive eating patterns. The nutritionist will be able to help you correct negative thoughts and feelings about food and weight, and she will teach you healthy eating habits and weight management skills. Again, be sure to ask the nutritionist how much experience she has had with addictive eaters.

IS HOSPITAL TREATMENT RIGHT FOR YOU?

Most hospital treatment programs for eating disorders last about 30 days. If you are unable to function in your world, too depressed to go to work or get out of bed, are at medical risk because your weight is dangerously low or you are unable to stop purging around the clock, you will benefit from inpatient care. In the hospital you will receive medical and psychological supervision. These programs are very expensive, but many health insurance policies will cover hospitalization.

Don't think that you will be totally cured after a 30-day stay. Hospital treatment is only a time out from your crisis situation. When you are released, all the situations and relationships that contributed to your anxiety and depression will still be waiting for you. Recovery from food addiction is a gradual process of uncovering and resolving difficult emotional issues underlying the eating disorder. Treatment may take a year or more. Your recovery is complete when food and weight obsessions are ended and self-esteem and self-acceptance are restored.

A good hospital program is comprehensive and includes medical, psychological and nutritional counseling. Individual and group or family therapy should be mandatory. The best program will require you to continue outpatient psychotherapy in order to continue the progress begun in the hospital. Some of the inpatient programs are modeled after the twelve step program of Overeaters Anonymous, others are not. Before you enter a hospital program you may want to shop around and compare the types of treatment offered and the qualifications of the staff who will be working with you.

Whatever therapeutic experiences you choose, you will find new awareness and change that sooner or later will help you to overcome binge eating. I have found that a combination of therapeutic modes seems to work best. I stress behavior therapy as a beginning step because any behavior change is valuable reinforcement and support for continuing the work. Transactional analysis and cognitive therapy help build understanding and provide winning concepts for change. Psychosynthesis, a creative therapy that uses art, music, and guided fantasy, can also provide a powerful base for change. Group therapy with its shared experiences and group support is especially helpful in overcoming self-defeating behaviors. There are no right and wrong choices about how to proceed. Take the first step, and you will find yourself with new options for health.

ADVICE TO FAMILY AND FRIENDS

If you have a loved one who is caught up in the problem of addictive eating, you may be frustrated by your inability either to understand or to help that person. You may be dealing with an anorectic, a bulimic, a compulsive over-eater, or someone who has a problem with food that you can't seem to categorize. Many family members or spouses have tried bribery, tricks, threats, punishment, cajoling, pleading, denying, or ignoring the problem—but none of these will work.

All food abusers are having trouble with relationships. Some of those relationships involve you. There are two pitfalls in relating—being a persecutor and being a rescuer. If you try to make the person change by punishment, verbal abuse, or being a policeman, you set her up to react to or rebel against your power. This pattern can go on for years without positive results. Your displeasure may temporarily put the binger in her place, but she will also feel resentment toward your commands and find ways, sometimes passive or subtle, to flaunt your wishes.

When you comment verbally or nonverbally with facial expressions concerning disappointment or displeasure at what the food addict is doing, you are not helping; you are heaping shame upon a person who is more critical of herself than you could ever be. The pressure you put on her to improve may add insult to injury.

Many family members and friends think they are being loving or helpful when they are really carrying out a rescue operation. Rescuing is never helpful when the one you love is already fully capable of doing it herself if she chooses to. Overprotecting the food abuser, trying to help her avoid conflict, or backing down so as not to upset the "sick" individual will tend to keep her powerless and a perpetual victim. The person with an eating disorder may actively seek out someone who will take care of her. When that person comes along, the binger will both love and hate the rescuer. At first she will be grateful to be free of the burden of responsibility, but later she will grow to resent the rescuer, who seems to make himself out to be "better than" the binger. I recall a client telling me she went out to dinner with a close friend. When they ordered, the friend made sure to tell the waitress to eliminate the bread from my client's dinner because she could not "handle" bread. My client, a thirty-year-old woman, could very well have told the waitress herself what she wanted.

I will share with you what I tell all my adult clients: *What you eat and how you eat it is nobody else's business, but it is your business!*

There are people who seem to need relationships in which they can nurture or "save" an unfortunate other. Food addicts are often drawn to lovers who seem to enjoy being helpers. After a while, however, the binger may feel like the underdog, continuously not OK, always striving to be perfect in order to deserve love, but not making it. Resentment will lead to repeated binging out of anger at feeling put down or criticized. In the relationship of a victim and rescuer, trouble ensues when the victim starts to get better and no longer needs rescuing. What does a rescuer do when there is nobody to rescue?

A husband of a bulimic was worried because he had just learned how tormented his wife was around food. They went out to eat every weekend. He was afraid that he was the cause of her purging because he brought her into contact with temptation. I suggested that he give his wife the choice of where to go: dinner, a movie, a drive, or another activity. He replied, "Oh, she'll say, 'Whatever you want, dear." He needs to learn ways to encourage her to make choices and not accept the non-choice of going along with whatever others want. One powerful way is to insist that the other person make a choice. If she decides to people-please she must be informed of her responsibility in accepting the consequences of her choice. It is always valuable to be direct and honest about your thoughts and feelings. Many anorectics and bulimics do a mind-reading act. They think they know how you feel and what you want and deny their own needs to fill yours.

There is nothing wrong with talking openly to those close to you about your doubts and fears concerning their condition. Jamie always overate and threw up after eating at her mother's house. Her mother often served rich casseroles which Jamie told herself were "bad" or "fattening." She was afraid that if she turned down food, her mother would worry that she had reverted to her former anorectic behavior. Because she did not want to upset her mother, she continued to eat in a way that would reassure her mother but would ensure continued vomiting. If her mother had been able to talk out loud about her obvious fears for her twenty-five-year-old daughter, they could have gotten closer to each other. Neither mother nor daughter was able to have open communication. Everything was done by assumption and wishful thinking. Mother continued to scare herself with fear about Jamie without talking to Jamie. Jamie continued to try to find ways to behave "normally" to assuage her mother's fear, all the while continuing to hate herself for being bulimic. Each was rescuing the other, and neither was happy.

Persecutors are people who inflict guilt trips on the binge eater by making her responsible for the persecutor's well-being. This was the situation with Francine, whose mother had a bad heart. Whenever Francine did something her mother disapproved of, her mother would say, "You'll be the death of me." This did not stop Francine from overeating, but it made her more guilty about hating the mother she was supposed to love. Glen's wife would assault him with, "How can you do this? If you really loved me, you would lose weight/stop throwing up/get over this problem." No amount of scare or threat will deter a binge eater. The anorectic, bulimic, or compulsive overeater is not binging or purging to hurt you, although if she knows that it bothers you it becomes a tempting way of manipulating or punishing you in the long run.

I have dealt with many overweight women who, as victims, marry men who announced before the wedding that they hated fat people. The victim and persecutor then spend the next ten, twenty, or thirty years playing a game. He picks on her for her weight, and she gets back at him by eating even more.

A problem with being a policeman is that you must constantly judge the other. But the words *good* and *bad* are unproductive, tending to keep the food abuser in a state of guilt and fear. The result is that the binge eater will maintain even more secrecy, and that will increase her feelings of powerlessness in the face of compulsion. Instead of the word *bad*, use the word *anxious* or *stressed*. Instead of *good*, say *in charge of your choices or powerful*.

UNDERSTANDING THE PROBLEM

It may be impossible for you to put yourself into the shoes of the binge eater. If you have never had a food problem or experienced a compulsion, you tell yourself that the individual in question just has to use more willpower or determination to shape up and kick the bad habit. Yet almost everyone has a self-defeating habit that is troublesome and difficult to overcome. Thousands of people are burdened by excessive shyness, or are plagued by fear of heights, flying, or driving.

This was the case of a couple who came to see me. The wife of one of my clients came for counseling with her husband because, after fifteen years of watching him try to diet and stop binging, she was "ready to give up on him." She had no food hang-ups and could not relate to her spouse's problem. But she did have her own non-constructive habit. Her self-defeating behavior involved a lack of motivation. For her to be more successful at her selling job, she had to make more calls, but she hated using the phone because she feared rejection from potential clients.

She realized that her inner conflicts and fears about success and failure, about self-worth and lovability stopped her from achieving her goal. I helped her see that her husband went through a similar sequence of feelings and actions——but with food. Once she understood that all self-defeating behaviors had much in common, she was able to change her judgment of her husband and understand that he was dealing with more than a bad habit.

Before you condemn the binge eater, take some time to think about your own shortcomings. Are you perfect? What behavior would you like to change in yourself? Think about how often you have thought about or tried to change. How successful were you? *Everyone is doing his or her very best at all times.* If you could do better, you would do better! When you are not doing what you "should," the answer is to find out how you stop yourself, not punish yourself for your mistakes.

Remember, a food abuser, like any other human, is neither good nor bad. Binge behavior is a sign of emotional overload. Each binger is lacking—not in willpower—but in effective means of dealing with her life's situations that cause intense feelings, either happy or unhappy.

Most food addicts are starving for attention and affection. The binger tells herself that she is unworthy or ugly because of her "nasty habit" and will shy away from social contact. She usually does not ask for closeness from another because she thinks it must either be earned by being perfect (and she never achieves perfection) or it doesn't count if she has to ask for a hug or a good word.

A POSITIVE APPROACH

Whenever possible, find ways to praise or compliment your friend. Do not focus on his or her food or weight, but keep in mind that she is really a lovable and capable human being, with many talents and extraordinary traits. In addition to verbal reinforcement, physical touch is an important nonverbal way of being supportive. Physical contact is important to all people. Whenever I treat widows or single or divorced people who live alone, I suggest that they try to find activities that will help them "rub shoulders" or "hold hands' with others. Folk or square dancing, classes in massage or acupressure help individuals to receive much needed physical caring in a safe, non-sexual atmosphere. Don't forget hugs. Pats on the back, back rubs, a squeeze on the arm are all ways of giving affection.

THE VALUE OF PSYCHOTHERAPY

In therapy, the binge eater must deal with her behavior along with many other underlying factors. Don't expect that the health professional will "fix" your friend or loved one in six weeks or six months. The best way to help is to stay out of this area of your friend's efforts at recovery. Simply share your caring feelings and allow her the respect that she can reveal about her therapy whatever she chooses.

On the other hand, if you are invited to attend psycho-therapy with the food abuser, you may find that both of you benefit greatly from the experience. In cases of anorexia nervosa, family therapy is an important aspect of recovery. Bulimics and compulsive overeaters have many unresolved issues that they would like to deal with concerning mother, father, or other family members. When the spouse of a person with an eating disorder participates in marital counseling, the problem eater makes changes faster than if she were tackling the problem alone. The therapy office is a neutral, safe place where people can learn to practice new communication techniques and talk about stressful feelings. Often, the spouse of a binge eater is amazed by what his wife reveals, even though they have been married for many years. The therapist's office is like a classroom where old problems or conflicts can be brought up and then let go of. New tools for the relation-ship can be acquired. In this way, the food abuser can learn more effective skills to cope with problems and also ways to change stressful behavior and thinking patterns.

UNCONDITIONAL ACCEPTANCE

One of the most important pieces of advice to the family and friends of a person with an eating disorder is, *you cannot fix the other person!* Although you may worry about her health and even her life, you do not have the training or know-how to make anyone better. You can, however, give one thing that nobody else can—you can give uncon-ditional acceptance. That is the most meaningful quality of relationship that everyone wants.

"Unconditional acceptance" means that you see past the weight changes, the binges, the purges, the pain, and the conflict of that anorectic, bulimic, or compulsive overeater to the true self within. You let her do what she has to do without blaming, shaming, or discounting her feelings. Unconditional acceptance is saying, "I love you even though I don't love what you are doing."

It is very hard to separate the behavior from the real nature of the person. You may need help in achieving this. Perhaps you will look for a support group or enter therapy to sort out your feelings and learn new ways to express your love.

Like many others, you may love the binger yet find that you do not know how to control your feelings of frustration and worry. There are two harmful kinds of communication that helping friends often get caught in when there is an emotional crisis: blaming and discounting.

Blaming happens when you are upset because you can't help the other or fix the situation. In your frustration, you turn to the food abuser and say things like, "You deserve that" or "What can you expect when you do something so stupid?" The binger is doing the best she can. She may get herself into many unpleasant or unhappy scrapes because of her difficulty in liking herself or in handling feelings of anxiety. When you disapprove or doubt the other, you are not helping her to see the problem or solve it; you are stimulating emotional reactions of guilt, anger, and resentment.

Instead of blaming, perhaps you can learn to say, "I feel powerless to help you when you do _____" and "When you tell me about your problem, I wish I could make everything nice for you, but I can't." It is permissible to share your feelings of frustration and powerlessness, and even to reveal the urge to blame, but let the other person know that you want to understand. Ask the food addict what she thinks you can do to help. Do not offer solutions, telling the binger what you think she should do. When you take over and fix things, the person with the problem is not required to be responsible for the actions that get her into this position in the first place.

The second harmful type of interaction is discounting. A discount is a comment or behavior in which one person belittles the feelings of the other. You may be a discounter and not know it. Common discount statements are, "Don't be silly!" and "How can you feel that way?" Do you make remarks like that? You may think that you respect the other individual, yet you are not demonstrating to her that you understand her feelings. You think to yourself that if you were in that place, you wouldn't feel scared or overwhelmed or upset. But your friend is not you, and you are not her. Feelings do not have to be defended! To disagree with another's feelings is like telling a person who is thirsty, "Stop that right now!" If you are thirsty, you can't turn it off. If you are angry or sad, you can't stop those feelings on command. When you try to help a friend by telling her that her unhappiness or compulsion is silly or bad, you are judging her. That is the last thing she wants to hear.

HOW YOU CAN HELP

Jean Rubel, founder of ANRED (Anorexia Nervosa And Related Eating Disorders) in Eugene, Oregon, encourages friends or classmates of food abusers who won't get help to recruit other important people to talk to her. Even if someone has sworn you to secrecy, if you keep the promise, you may be harming your friend more than helping her. Enlist the aid of parents, family members, employer, co-workers, school counselors or nurses. Your friend will probably become angry with you now, but later she may thank you for getting her help when she couldn't get it for herself.

It is important to set limits to take care of yourself and the rest of your family, roommates or circle or friends. Here is a list of DON'TS suggested by ANRED:

1. Don't let the food addict abuse your generosity in service of her food addiction.
2. Don't let her steal your food.
3. Don't lend her money to support her binge or binge/purge habit.
4. Don't loan her your car if you know she is going to buy binge food.
5. Don't let her mess up the kitchen or bathroom and expect you to clean it.

Although you can't fix the other person, you do not have to bear the burden of her recovery either. That leaves you free to be a real friend. All you have to do is listen. There is an art to listening. When your friend tells you her problems and her misery, do you find your thoughts wandering as you make up rebuttals of "Yes but" or "Why don't you . . ." as she goes along? Do you spend time trying to solve her problem as she talks? You do not have to do that because you are not her doctor or psychologist.

All you have to do to be a good listener is to be attentive to her words and repeat what she is saying back to her, in your own words. You may add what you think your friend is feeling, but do not psychoanalyze or judge, just be a mirror reflecting what is projected onto you.

For example, if a binge eater tells you that she is miserable because she just paid $300 to join a diet program and yet she keeps binging, refrain from saying, "Why don't you use willpower?" Instead say, "I can hear how unhappy you are about not being able to stay on your diet. I guess you feel as if you wasted a lot of money." Then let her respond. When you respond, you reflect her words and feelings. Keep up this interchange until the other person has come up with some thoughts or ideas to help herself. She may finish by realizing that she has not failed and can continue to work on her problem until she achieves her goal. You will discover that you are less stressed than when you felt responsible for helping and solving the binger's problems.

The future is uncertain. The one you love may not recover; she may get better and have relapses or she may overcome her problem. You cannot predict what will happen; nor can you designate how long it will take for her to heal. The more expectations you have, the more pressure you are putting on her to meet your needs. Can you accept this individual as he or she is today? (She may never change.) If you cannot love the other as he or she is with her problem, you are not going to be a positive force in helping her help herself. Perhaps at that point, you might need to remove yourself from the relationship.

If you are determined to stand by your friend or family member, here are some things you will need to think about and practice:

1. Stop trying to "fix" the other person.
2. Encourage the food addict to find professional help.
3. Understand the problem by reading or consulting with an expert.
4. Recognize food abuse as a sign or symptom of other conflicts in the person's life that he or she is not coping with.
5. Avoid discounting or belittling the other's feelings.
6. Avoid policing or persecuting.
7. Avoid rescuing or backing down when there is conflict.
8. Learn how to listen in a loving way.
9. Practice unconditional acceptance.

One of the driving forces that compels families to pressure the addict is fear. Severe complications arise from anorexia and bulimia. Many people are afraid that the problem eater will die. Many are afraid because they fear behavior that is irrational. If you try to frighten the anorectic or bulimic, you will find yourself in the midst of a power struggle. The more you insist, the more she will resist change.

If the anorectic or bulimic is an adolescent, you, as the parent, have the responsibility of seeking medical help. If the person is an adult, you cannot coerce her, but you can discuss the problem in a clear way, expressing your concern and providing information that you may have about the nature of the problem, the side effects, and the possibilities for change. Again, the final decision for an adult will be determined by her own desire to overcome the problem.

Many parents of binge eaters and some spouses think that they are to blame for the other's eating disorder. Please remember that most people do the best that they can. Sometimes parents were not well parented themselves, and they bring those deficits to the parenting of their own children. If you feel as if you are to blame, you need to understand your actions and feelings from a new point of view in order to forgive yourself. Family therapy is often very helpful in healing the confused feelings that arise when a child becomes troubled with an eating disorder.

In addition to guilt, the parent or lover of a binge eater may also feel anger toward the person with the problem. Sometimes this anger can add to the guilt. It is often expressed: "How can you be angry with a sick person?" You can, and often should express anger as a valid statement of concern and love. Many binge eaters have used their food issues as a battleground to work out power struggles with loved ones. Sometimes a family member will feel angry at that person because he tells himself, "If she loved me, she would get better."

If you are plagued with guilt or anger toward the anorectic, bulimic, or compulsive overeater, you need to understand yourself better in relation to the problem. The person with the disorder is usually not going to get better to please you. That may be the trouble! Most food addicts are fighting against being people-pleasers. Chances are that you did not cause the problem nor can you make it go away.

Your relationship with the person with an eating disorder may be in conflict. This conflict adds to her anxiety. But it is her responsibility to recognize and learn to do something about it. You may help by taking a look at your relationship with her. Stop blaming yourself or the other and gain new insight into the dynamics of your interactions! When a couple or family of a food abuser come for counseling, they often discover that they care deeply about each other but have not been able to tell or show their love in ways that the other understands. When they are able to cut through the anger and frustration, they find that there is a bond of love that has always been there but got covered up and forgotten. The expression of love and caring, newly realized, often brings about changes in other behaviors.

LOVING AND FORGIVING

Whether you are the parent of a small child and want to avoid future eating problems or the parent or friend of an adult with an eating problem, the message to you is the same. There are two important points to remember: love and forgive. The hardest thing in the world is to give up your expectation of another and love her with total acceptance—loving her as she is now. Letting go does not mean walking away. It means being supportive without either criticizing or rescuing. You may need help in learning to achieve this state of peaceful acceptance and may want to join a support group like Al Anon for people like you or you may decide to find a therapist who specializes in family counseling.

Forgiveness is another essential quality that you will need to cultivate. Both you and the addicted eater may have many old hurts and angers that need to be cleared away. When you form a vacuum by cleaning out the garbage of the past, you make room for something new and beautiful to fill that place within you. I have a fantasy of a wonderful scene of a group on a hill on a sunny day. Each person would express to the other the specific hurt or anger that she has been hanging on to. She would say, "I now let go of my anger about _____." Each one would then write each anger on an inflated balloon. After all the angers and hurts are inscribed, the balloons would be let go to fly away while participants celebrated.

Every person alive has shortcomings or problems of some kind. Yet each of us wants to be loved and accepted as the basically decent person, the essence of a special soul, which dwells beneath the surface turmoil. The food addict is very much like you. The only difference lies in the choice and style of coping with emotions and life's problems. In helping to understand and love her, you will be learning to accept and love yourself.

STOP ADDICTIVE EATING! THE 4-LEVEL PLAN

Addictive eating begins as a *solution* to a problem. Eventually taking on a life of its own, the behavior becomes the problem.

A compulsive act is an intense emotional statement. It is a symbolic cry for help. When you decode that message behind your behavior, you will be able to eliminate food abuse from your life.

Examine the dynamics of your addictive eating behavior. When you become familiar with the triggers, the situations and relationships that cause you to feel helpless, victimized, frustrated, or angry, you will soon become aware of the problem as it is happening. Then you can do something about it before you act compulsively.

1. PHYSICAL LEVEL . . . Behavior

Keep a diary in which you identify compulsive episodes of binging and/or purging. Rate each on an intensity scale of 1 to 10 as if it were an earthquake.

2. EMOTIONAL LEVEL . . . Feelings

For each compulsive act, ask yourself: "What in my live is a 7.9 or a 9.5?" What situation or relationship is involved? Be specific. What strong feelings arose from that situation or experience (Mad, Glad, Sad, Scared)?

3. COGNITIVE LEVEL . . . Thoughts and beliefs

What did you tell yourself about that upsetting situation that caused you to feel angry, frustrated, helpless or guilty? (*"Ain't it awful, and there's nothing I can do about it." "Everyone is better than me." "What will people think?" "If you loved me you would . . . "*)

4. TRANSPERSONAL LEVEL . . . Retrieving your power

How can you stop making yourself feel like a victim?

1) **Take Action**: If the situation or relationship is extremely harmful to you, what can you do to change it now?

2) **Changing Your Attitude**: Are your thoughts and beliefs irrational and "twisted"? What can you tell yourself about the difficult situation or relationship that would lead to more positive and satisfying feelings?

SUGGESTED READINGS

Arenson, Gloria. *How To Stop Playing the Weighting Game*. New York: St. Martin's Press, 1981.

Assagioli, Roberto. *Psychosynthesis*. New York: Viking, 1971.

_____. *Act of Will*. New York: Viking, 1973.

Beck, Aaron T. *Cognitive Therapy and the Emotional Disorders*. New York: Meridian, 1976.

Beller, Anne S. *Fat and Thin: A Natural History of Obesity*. New York: McGraw Hill, 1977.

Bradshaw, John. *Healing the Shame that Binds You*. Deerfield Beach, FL: Health Communications, 1988.

Bruch, Hilde. *Eating Disorders: Obesity, Anorexia Nervosa, and the Person Within*. New York: Basic Books, 1973.

_____. *The Golden Cage*. Cambridge, MA: Harvard University Press, 1988.

Burns, David D. *Feeling Good: The New Mood Therapy*. New York: Morrow, 1980.

Chernin, Kim. *The Obsession: Reflections on the Tyranny Of Slenderness*. New York: Harper & Row, 1981.

Emery, Gary *et al. New Directions in Cognitive Therapy*. New York: Guilford Press, 1981.

Goleman, Daniel. *Vital Lies, Simple Truths*. New York: Simon & Schuster, 1985.

Hatterer, Lawrence J. *The Pleasure Addicts*. New York: A.S. Barnes, 1980.

Hodgson, Ray and Peter Miller. *Self Watching*. New York: Facts on File, 1982.

James, Muriel and Dorothy Jongeward. *Born to Win*. Reading, MA: Addison-Wesley, 1971.

Jongeward, Dorothy. *Women as Winners*. Reading, MA: Addison-Wesley, 1976.

Keyes, Elizabeth. *How to Win the Losing Fight*. Denver, CO: Gentle Living Publications, 1952.

Kupfermann, Jeanette. *The MsTaken Body*. Great Britain: Robson, 1979.

Lazarus, Arnold and Allen Fay. *I Can if I Want To*. New York: Warner Books, 1975.

Levenkron, Steven. *Treating and Overcoming Anorexia Nervosa*. New York: Charles Scribner's Sons, 1982.

Marlatt, G. Alan and Judith Gordon. *Relapse Prevention*. New York: Guilford Press, 1985.

Milkman, Harvey and Stanley Sunderwirth. *Craving for Ecstasy*. Lexington, MA: Lexington Books, 1987

Offit, Avodah. *Night Thoughts: Reflections of a Sex Therapist*. New York: Congdon and Lattes, 1981.

Orbach, Susie. *Fat is a Feminist Issue*. New York: Paddington, 1978.

_____. *Hunger Strike*. New York: W.W. Norton, 1986.

Phelps, Janice Keller, M.D. and Alan E. Nourse, M.D. *The Hidden Addiction and How to Get Free*. Boston: Little, Brown and Co., 1986.

Ray, Sondra. *The Only Diet There Is*. Millbrae, CA: Celestial Arts, 1981.

Schaef, Ann Wilson. *When Society Becomes an Addict*. San Francisco: Harper & Row, 1987.

Vincent, L.M. *Competing with the Sylph: Dancers and the Pursuit of the Ideal Body Form*. New York: Andrew and McMeel, 1980.

White, Marlene B. and William C. White. *Bulimarexia: The Binge/Purge Cycle*. New York: W.W. Norton, 1983.

Woodman, Marion. *The Owl was a Baker's Daughter: Obesity, Anorexia Nervosa, and the Repressed Feminine*. Toronto: Inner City Books, 1980.

INDEX